Walking
Notorious London

Walking Notorious *London*

ANDREW DUNCAN

FROM GUNPOWDER PLOT TO GANGLAND: WALKS THROUGH LONDON'S DARK HISTORY

PASSPORT BOOKS
NTC/Contemporary Publishing Group

This edition first published in 2001
by Passport Books, a division of
NTC/Contemporary Publishing Group, Inc.
4255 West Touhy Avenue
Lincolnwood (Chicago), Illinois 60712-1975
U.S.A.

ISBN 0-658-01612-1

Library of Congress Catalog Card Number: on file
Published in conjunction with New Holland Publishers (UK) Ltd

Publishing Manager: Jo Hemmings
Editor: Pete Duncan
Copy-editor: Paul Barnett
Editorial Assistant: Jo Cleere
Design, page layout, cartography and index: Hardlines, Charlbury

Reproduction by Pica Colour Separation Overseas (Pte) Ltd, Singapore
Printed and bound in Singapore by Kyodo Printing Co. (Singapore) Pte Ltd

Photographic Acknowledgements
All photographs by the author with the exception of the following:
Camera Press plates 13, 21, 35; Hulton Getty Picture Collection plates 16, 19, 20, 26, 27,
31; Mary Evans Picture Library plates 5, 7, 8, 10, 12, 15, 17, 22, 29, 30, 32, 33, 34; David
Paterson front cover, back cover, plates 1, 4, 11, 18, 23, 24, 36.

Front cover: Walker's Court, Soho (David Paterson).
Back cover: Raven at the Tower of London (David Paterson).
Spine: Detail from House of Detention Museum (Andrew Duncan).

Contents

Key to Maps

Each of the walks in this book is accompanied by a detailed map on which the route is shown in purple. Places of interest along the walks are clearly identified, and places open to the public are underlined.

At the beginning of the text for each walk there is information on transport (the walks start and finish at underground stations) and refreshments.

Opening times are listed chapter by chapter at the back of the book, starting on page 151.

The following is a key to symbols and abbreviations used on the maps:

Symbols

- route of walk
- railway line
- major building
- † church
- public toilets
- park
- Underground
- railway station

Abbreviations

APP	Approach	PH	Public House
AVE	Avenue	(Pub)	
CLO	Close	PK	Park
COTTS	Cottages	PL	Place
CT	Court	RD	Road
DRI	Drive	S	South
E	East	SQ	Square
GDNS	Gardens	ST	Street
GRN	Green	STN	Station
GRO	Grove	TER	Terrace
HO	House	UPR	Upper
LA	Lane	VW	View
LWR	Lower	W	West
MS	Mews	WD	Wood
MT	Mount	WHF	Wharf
N	North	WLK	Walk
PAS	Passage	WY	Way
PDE	Parade		

Introduction

London has such a rich past – and present – that one could pick almost any aspect and make a book out of it. In this case I have chosen – as the fourth in my series of guides to the city – to focus on the notorious side of life in the capital's teeming streets. The thrust of the book is mainly historical, but there is a lot of 20th-century material in it, particularly gangland bosses, prostitution and the porn trade in the East End and Soho, while, in the case of the Westminster chapter, which features a number of political scandals, some of the people and events described are of a very recent date. So, whether you are interested in the notorious London of old or of today, you should find something in this book to titillate your taste buds.

'Notorious' is a broad umbrella term, and I have applied it liberally to many different people, places and events. Generally speaking, anything to do with murder, theft, swindle, fraud, bribery, corruption, blackmail, sex, scandal, pornography, prostitution, adultery, gambling, spying, violence, prisons, executions, torture and squalor gets a mention. There are probably other categories represented in this book, but I think that's enough to be going on with for the time being!

The structure of the book is based on the premise that, at different times, the main areas of central London have all been notorious for one reason or another. Each area has its own chapter, and the chapters are arranged broadly from east to west. Each chapter starts with an introductory feature focusing on what it is that has made the area notorious – for example, in the East End it was Jack the Ripper in the 19th century and the Kray brothers in the 20th century – and continues with a walk. The walk passes sites associated with the main theme of the chapter as well as others associated with the overall notorious theme of the book.

One final point. There aren't – perhaps for obvious reasons – many places in London associated with its notorious past or present which are open to the public. But anywhere that is is highlighted in bold type in the text and underlined on the relevant map. Opening times are listed in alphabetical order of venue in a separate section at the end of the book.

If you have any comments on this or any of my other books, please e-mail them to me at andrew@andrewduncan.co.uk. For details of my other books please check out my website at www.andrewduncan.co.uk

I hope you have fun on the walks – and take care not to become part of London's notorious past yourself!

Andrew Duncan

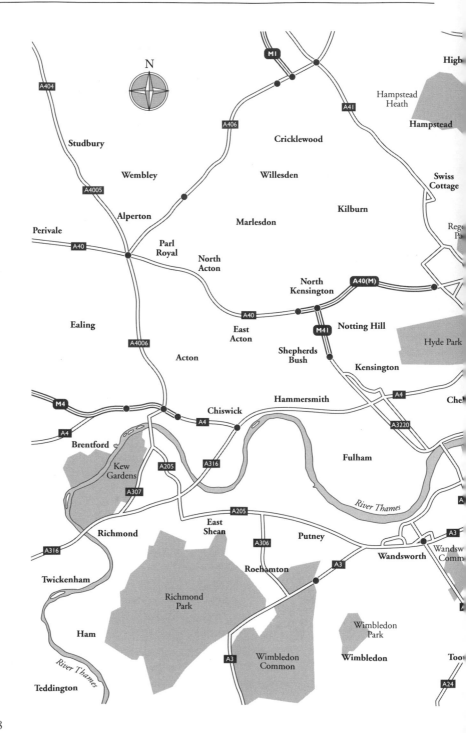

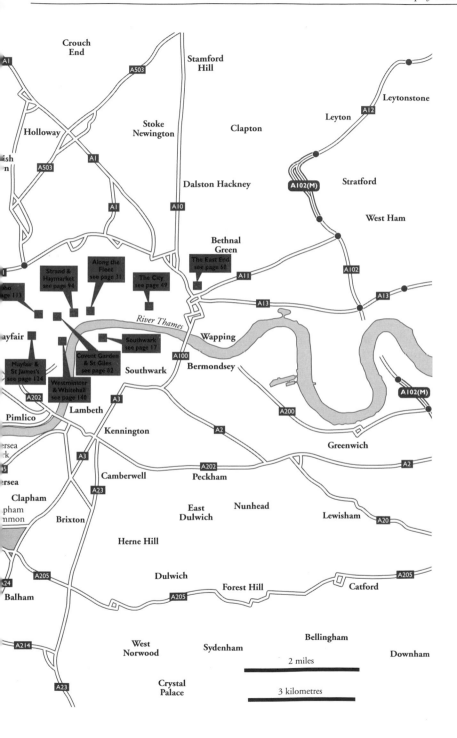

Southwark

Brothels and Bloodsports

In the Middle Ages what we today call London consisted of the two distinct cities of London and Westminster plus, on the south side of the river, the suburb of Southwark.

Southwark generally had an unsavoury reputation as a haunt of criminals and low-life. It was close to the City but outside its control, and criminals found it easy to nip across to the Borough, as the area was generally called, either via London Bridge or by boat. Once there, there were rich pickings amongst the travellers in the inns lining the High Street and the customers of the numerous local brothels. Law enforcement here was lax, mainly due to the fact that Southwark was divided up into no fewer than five competing jurisdictions. If you did happen to fall foul of the law you could take refuge in one of several sanctuaries in the area, notably Paris Garden. Here, provided you paid your 4d entry fee and had your name and crime recorded in the sanctuary register, you were free from arrest for up to 40 days.

But there was one part of Southwark which was more notorious than all the rest: Bankside. Bankside, as its name suggests, was (and still is) part of the riverside area of Southwark. Throughout the Middle Ages it consisted mainly of a string of brothels – or stews as they were called, from 'stewhouses', meaning hot-bath houses – which constituted London's main red-light district. After the stews were shut down in the mid-16th century, other amusements replaced them, notably bear-, bull- and other forms of animal-baiting and, of course, the theatre. With 'immoral' theatres banned in the puritan City, Bankside became Tudor London's main theatre district – everything banned in the City ended up in Southwark. At a time when actors (even ones as eminent as Shakespeare) were seen as little better than rogues and vagabonds, this was not exactly something the elders of Southwark would have been delighted about.

The introduction to this chapter focuses on Bankside and the highly dubious amenities it offered Londoners through half a millennium of whoring, drinking, fighting, gambling, play-acting and animal torture. The walk covers both Bankside – which today features a modern reconstruction of its most famous Tudor theatre, Shakespeare's Globe – and notorious sites in Southwark generally, including the royal prisons of the Marshalsea and the King's Bench, two of old London's most terrible gaols.

The Bankside Stews

Medieval London had several red-light districts, including the aptly-named Cock Lane in Smithfield. But by far the biggest and most notorious was Bankside, across the river in Southwark. Here there were some eighteen brothels strung out along the riverside facing the centre of the City. Viewed from the City they stood out clearly because of their whitewashed fronts and the fact that their signs were mounted flat on their fronts instead of at right-angles, as they would have been in a normal street. If you wanted to get to them from the City you either went across London Bridge and turned right or took a boat from the bottom of Stews Lane to Bankside Stairs.

No one knows who started the Bankside stews or when, but two things seem clear. One is that, though called stews, they do not appear actually to have been hot-bath houses. Probably the name was an import from the Continent, where the connection between bath houses and brothels had been close since Roman times. (Ironically, the connection did become close in London too, but not until the 18th century, when Turkish-style bagnios doubled up as houses of assignation, as you will see in the Covent Garden chapter.) The other thing we know about the stews is that they were certainly in existence by 1161: in that year, in a parliament held at Westminster, King Henry II enacted a set of rules which defined how the Bankside stews were to be run. Quite why the King of England should have been involved in the regulation of a collection of brothels in a rather remote part of his capital is not exactly clear at the distance of nearly 1000 years, but it was presumably something to do with the unusual fact that the Bankside brothels were state-regulated. Officially regulated brothels were relatively common on the Continent – Henry II himself, in his capacity as Duke of Normandy, owned some in Rouen – but in England they were virtually unknown. In fact, apart from another set at the south-coast port town of Sandwich, the ones at Bankside were the only brothels of their kind in the country.

Henry's rules had two aims. One was to protect all parties involved in the stews: the stewmongers who ran them, the prostitutes who worked in them, and the men who used them; for example, the prostitutes in the Bankside stews could not be made to work there against their will, and they could not be forced to stay if they chose to leave. Henry's other aim was to ensure that the stews posed no threat to public order. So you could not get alcohol (or even food) in them; they were shut on holy days (except at lunchtimes); and, most importantly, they operated only during daylight hours. In fact, they were more like offices than anything else, with the prostitutes renting their rooms (at three times the market rent of 14d a week), servicing their clients and then departing to their homes at the end of the working day.

The Bankside stews were located in a little private jurisdiction with the quaint name of the Liberty of the Clink. This was a kind of medieval manor, and had its own manorial court and manorial prison, the Clink, from which we get our colloquial expression 'in the clink'. Anyone who broke the rules of the stews found themselves hauled before the court and, if convicted, perhaps sentenced to a spell in the Clink. John Sandes, for example, owner of the Castle stewhouse on Bankside, was brought before the Clink court in 1506 for opening his house on a holy day and allowing prostitutes to live in. It is not known whether he was 'clinked' as a punishment. The remains of the Clink prison and the site of the Castle stewhouse – now the riverside Anchor pub – feature on the walk.

Throughout the time the stews existed the Liberty of the Clink belonged to the Church, and more particularly to the Bishops of Winchester. For 400 years, therefore, you had the extraordinary situation of London's main red-light district being closely associated with the Roman Catholic Church. The medieval Church was of course deeply involved in regulating morals, but its attitude to prostitution was wholly pragmatic. Prostitution was regarded as saving lustful men from the greater sin of sodomy and society from the socially disruptive influences of 'lewd and incontinent' women, and was therefore seen as a necessary evil.

Bermondsey Abbey, near Southwark, granted the Liberty of the Clink to the Bishops of Winchester in 1107; the then bishop happened to be the brother of the king. At the east end of the riverside frontage of the 70-acre (28ha) estate, the bishops built themselves a large house to serve as their London base when they were in the capital on business. (The impressive ruins of the house are seen on the walk.) The stews stretched out along the riverside, literally only a stone's throw to the west.

To begin with the bishops probably owned all the stews. But as time went on they divested themselves of all but the freeholds of two, the Bell and the Barge. The rest passed into the hands of locals (there were seven stewmasters in late 13th century Southwark), grandees like William Walworth (the Lord Mayor of London who stabbed Wat Tyler, leader of the Peasants' Revolt – Tyler's followers had just destroyed Walworth's brothel), and institutions like the convent at Bow in east London. One hopes the head of the convent did not enquire too closely into the precise contents of her order's property portfolio!

In 1498 syphilis arrived in England. Prostitution had always been associated with other venereal diseases, like gonorrhoea – if you caught it from one of the Bankside whores, popularly known as Winchester geese, you were said to have been 'bitten by a Winchester goose'. The stews, however, were regularly inspected, so the disease problem never got out of hand. But syphilis was altogether more virulent and destructive than anything known before. Its rapid spread was probably the reason the Bankside stews were closed down in 1505 – although two-thirds of them were allowed to reopen the following year.

But, even without syphilis, the days of the stews were already numbered. Southwark was becoming an increasingly lawless place, largely, it was believed, because of the stews. Also, with the spread of the Reformation, moral attitudes were hardening. Eventually, on 13 April 1546, Henry VIII issued a proclamation announcing the immediate closure of the stews – and modern research has shown that this time they really did close. So ended, after an incredible four centuries of sex for sale, the great tradition of the Bankside stews, as much a part of London life as St Paul's or Dick Whittington or apprentice-day riots.

Gambling and Bear-Baiting

The closure of the stews paved the way for Bankside to become the main centre of dissipation in Tudor London. The process had already started at neighbouring Paris Garden, on the west side of Bankside. This was another private jurisdiction like the Liberty of the Clink. Up to the beginning of the 16th century it had been run as a criminals' sanctuary. Around 1530 William Baseley leased the Paris Garden manor house from its monastic owners, the Knights Hospitallers, and converted it into a public casino, with cards and dice and bowling alleys in the grounds. The new venture was so lucrative that, when Henry VIII acquired Paris Garden from the Hospitallers in 1536, he raised Baseley's rent more than fivefold, from £10 a year to £52.

On Bankside itself most of the old stews were converted into inns and taverns, leading one early 17th century writer to comment that it had become one continual alehouse. Prostitution continued, but illicitly and covertly rather than legally and openly as before. As poet John Taylor wrote:

> The stews in England bore a beastly sway
> Till eight Henry banished them away.
> And since these common whores were quite put down,
> A damned crew of private whores are grown.
> So that the devil will be doing still
> Either with public or with private ill.

In the gardens behind the old stews two theatres or rings for animal baiting were built, one on the site of the bishops' brothels, the Bell and the Barge. The baiting took place on Sunday afternoon and cost 1d to stand and 2d or more for a seat in the gallery. The main attractions were the baiting of bulls and bears by huge, half-starved mastiff dogs, well over a hundred of which were kept for the purpose in kennels at the back of the rings. The bulls and bears were roped or chained to a stake in the centre of the ring and then exposed to the full fury of the dogs, which of course attacked them from all sides.

Other attractions included the whipping of blind bears and also the baiting by dogs of a horse with a monkey riding on its back. 'It is a fine sight to see the horse run, kicking and biting, and the monkey grip the saddle tightly and scream, many times being bitten,' wrote a Venetian visitor to the Bankside baiting in 1562. The Spanish Duke of Najera thought that 'to see the pony kicking at the dogs and the ape shrieking at them as they hang on the ears and neck of the pony is enough to make you laugh'.

Queen Elizabeth would have agreed with the duke. She was a great fan of bear-baiting, and in 1559 brought the French ambassador to see the show, which was evidently one of the sights of the town. But not everybody was so fond of it, and many objectors saw the hand of God at work when eight people were killed after one of the stands at the bear-baiting ring collapsed in January 1583.

The Theatres

Some thirty years after bear-baiting got under way on Bankside, the City authorities made it pretty clear what they thought of plays and actors when they expelled the theatres from within the City wall. Loose-living Bankside was the ideal alternative venue, which is no doubt why no fewer than four new theatres came to be built there following the City's ban. Three were in the Liberty of the Clink – the Rose, the Globe (in which Shakespeare was both partner and actor) and the Hope – and one, the Swan, in Paris Garden. The Hope was built in 1613 on the site of the main bear-baiting ring, and with its removable stage, doubled up as both ring and theatre.

The golden age of the theatres did not last long on Bankside – only about twenty or thirty years – but it more than made up for this brevity with colour, excitement and vitality. During this brief golden age Bankside was at the height of its fame as a centre of pleasure and riotous living. Many of the leading theatre-owners, playwrights and actors – including, it is said, Shakespeare – lived on Bankside, and the area teemed with the kind of shiftless, devil-may-care types that are always attracted to red-light and entertainment districts.

Bear-Baiting Again

When the Puritans came to power during the Civil War in the 1640s, they shut down the theatres and the bear-baiting rings. The mastiff dogs were sent to Jamaica and the poor bears, with names like Samson and Harry Hunks, were executed by military firing squad. But after the restoration of the monarchy the previous incumbent of the post of Master of the Royal Bears, Bulls and Mastiff Dogs was restored to his position and allowed to rebuild the Bankside bear-baiting ring, this time with the extra amenity of an alehouse. Diarist John Evelyn went somewhat reluctantly to the new ring on 16 June 1670, by which time cock- and dog-fighting had been added to the bill:

> I was forced to accompany some friends to the Bear Garden where was cock-fighting, dog-fighting, bear and bull baiting, it being a famous day for all these butcherly sports or rather barbarous cruelties. The bulls did exceedingly well but the Irish wolf dog exceeded, which was a tall greyhound, a stately creature indeed, who beat a cruel mastiff. One of the bulls tossed a dog full into a lady's lap as she sat in one of the boxes at a considerable height from the arena. There were two poor dogs killed & so all ended with the ape on horseback, & I most heartily weary of the rude & dirty pastime, which I had not seen I think in twenty years before.

Samuel Pepys also visited the new ring. He thought it 'good sport' when, like Evelyn, he saw a bull toss a dog way up into a box, but concluded on balance that it was a 'rude and nasty pleasure'. He preferred to see the gladiatorial sword fights that had been a feature of the Bankside entertainments since at least 1603, when one famous fencer killed another by running him through the eye. On 27 May 1667 Pepys stood on a stool in the bear pit and watched a 'furious' fight between a butcher and a waterman. 'The former,' wrote Pepys,

> had the better all along, till by and by the latter dropped his sword out of his hand, and the butcher, whether not seeing his sword dropped or I know not, but did give him a cut over the wrist, so as he was disabled to fight any longer. But Lord, to see how in a minute the whole stage was full of watermen to revenge the foul play, and the butchers to defend their fellow, though most blamed him; and there they all fell to it, to knocking down and

cutting many of each side. It was pleasant to see, but
that I stood in the pit and feared that in the tumult
I might get some hurt. At last the rabble broke up,
and so I away to Whitehall.

Pepys and Evelyn were among the last people to enjoy, or at least
witness, the violent pleasures of Bankside. Bear-baiting continued in other
parts of London, as you will see in the next chapter, but Londoners were
increasingly looking west for their pleasure rather than south to
Southwark. Bankside had had its day.

THE SOUTHWARK WALK

Start and finish: Borough underground station (Northern line).
Length: 2½ miles (4km).
Refreshments: On the first leg of the walk (Borough High Street) there
are plenty of cafés, take-aways, pubs and restaurants, but the
highlight is the George, London's last surviving galleried
inn. On the second leg, along the riverside, there are three
pubs and a café. Here the highlight is the old Anchor pub,
at the beginning of Bankside and covering the site of the
Castle, one of the medieval Bankside stews. (Both George
and Anchor are shown on the map and pointed out on the
walk.) The final leg of the walk has an occasional
backstreet-type pub but is otherwise more or less bereft of
decent places to stop.

Come out of Borough station, turn left, and cross Marshalsea Road to Brandon
House. This modern office block stands on the site of the London home of the
Brandon family, hereditary keepers of the King's Bench Prison in the 15th and
16th centuries. Later the house became a royal mint and then a notorious
criminals' sanctuary, of which more towards the end of the walk.

Now cross Borough High Street to the steps of St George the Martyr
Church, turn left and then turn first right into the beginnings of Tabard Street.
Go into St George's Gardens on the left. You are now standing on the site of
the White Lion, one of old Southwark's five gaols. Established in a former inn
in the 1550s, the White Lion was for the 'murtherers, felons and other
notorious malefactors' of the county of Surrey, and was used until 1799. It was
then rebuilt as the new Marshalsea, the prison in which Charles Dickens's
parents were locked up as debtors and which he later immortalized in *Little
Dorrit* (1855–7) as 'an oblong pile of barrack building, partitioned into squalid
houses standing back to back environed by a narrow paved yard hemmed in by

high walls duly spiked at top'. A section of the wall survives on the far side of the garden. The old prison pump is in the **Cuming Museum**. Beyond the wall is the site of the King's Bench Prison.

Retrace your steps to Borough High Street and turn right, passing the London Institute of Technology and Research at 213 Borough High Street. This was part of the street frontage of the White Lion and the Marshalsea. Some time after the Marshalsea closed, a pub was built here called the

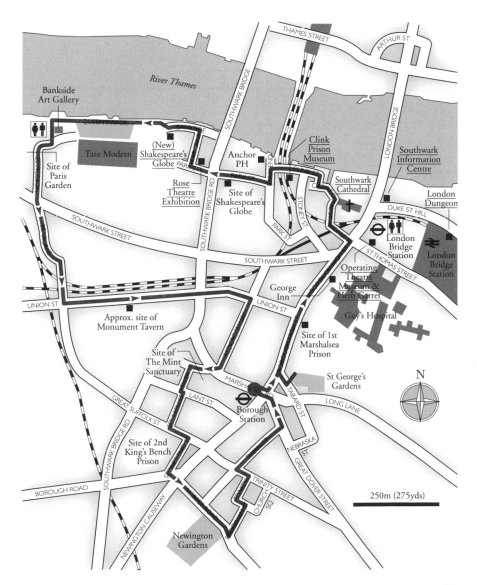

Crown (there is still a crown on the front of the building, right up at the top). At the turn of the century the landlord was poisoner George Chapman, whose third and last known victim, barmaid Maud Marsh, died here. Chapman, born in Poland as Severin Klosowski in 1865, was arrested in October 1902 and hanged at Wandsworth Prison the following April (see also page 66). Beyond the old Crown is (unsigned) Angel Place, a passage providing access to Southwark's local history library. Until 1758 it separated the White Lion prison from the King's Bench.

The King's Bench and Marshalsea, both opened around 1370, were royal prisons. Over time they evolved into notorious debtors' prisons characterized by corrupt administration and awful living conditions, at least for the vast majority of inmates (including whole families) who could not afford the keepers' exorbitant exactions. On balance the Marshalsea was probably worse than the King's Bench, but it was a happy day for all debtors when imprisonment for debt was finally abolished in the 19th century and these two scandalous hell-holes cleared away. (There is more about these prisons in the introductory feature to Chapter 2, which focuses on prisons and places of execution.)

Carry on along Borough High Street. Have a look to the right into Chapel Court. Half-timbered Lopex House, on the left, is how much of Southwark must have looked in Shakespeare's time, when it was at its most notorious. Just a little further along, on the right, a covered entrance leads into narrow Mermaid Court. On its left-hand side, between Mermaid Court and Newcomen Street, the original Marshalsea – described as an 'earthly hell' in 1718 – stood for a little over 400 years until its closure in 1811. The high wall on the left with barbed wire along the top, though nothing to do with the Marshalsea, is nonetheless a rather gruesome reminder of it.

Continue along Borough High Street. Somewhere hereabouts, on a site that has not yet been identified, there was in the late 18th century a pub called the Three Brewers. Highwayman Jerry Abershaw was enjoying a drink here one day in 1795 when a party of peace officers came to arrest him. Abershaw drew his pistols, killed one of the officers and wounded another, but was arrested and later hanged on Kennington Common, the scene of many of his exploits. He was only 22.

Just before you get to the war memorial, cross left to 54 Borough High Street, the office of Field and Sons, estate agents. Field and Sons started business in 1804 but didn't come here until 1876. The year before that the shop belonged to murderer Henry Wainwright's ironmonger brother Thomas (see page 71), and it was here that on 11 September 1875 Henry arrived with the dismembered body of his ex-mistress, intending to bury it in the basement. However, the police were waiting for him, and he was immediately arrested; he was hanged at Newgate on 21 December following, the first man to be executed in London for seven years. According to a brief history of the building in the window, long before Wainwright's time No 54 was a brothel staffed by rejects from Elizabeth Holland's more upmarket establishment at nearby Paris Garden. (The walk passes the site of this latter brothel shortly.)

Continue along the High Street, keeping on the pavement to the right of the war memorial. On this triangular site used to stand the local courthouse and prison called the Borough Compter (pronounced Counter), established after the City took control of Southwark in the 1550s. (Formerly the parish church had stood here – see the plaque low down on the corner of what used to be the old town hall.) Just ahead, you pass the entrance to a narrow alley called Counter Court, a relic of the old gaol which moved to another site, off Tooley Street, after Southwark's Great Fire of 1676. Looking right here you can see into the yard of the George, one of the pubs recommended in the *Refreshment* notes at the beginning of this walk. The George dates from the rebuilding of Southwark after the 1676 fire, and is the only one the numerous galleried inns built in Southwark at that time to survive.

Keep going along the High Street. At the lights, cross over to the NatWest bank in Southwark Street and turn right. At the junction look right towards the church in St Thomas Street. This was once the chapel of St Thomas's Hospital, which moved to Lambeth in 1862. Between about 1800 and 1830 both St Thomas's Hospital and neighbouring Guy's Hospital (which is still going, a little further down St Thomas Street) were the main customers of London's most notorious gang of bodysnatchers, the Borough Boys, led first by pock-marked Ben Crouch, son of a Guy's Hospital carpenter, and later by cool, calculating Irishman Patrick Murphy. Bodysnatching became big business in London from the 1770s onwards because the demand from the ever-growing number of student surgeons for bodies to dissect exceeded the legal supply of corpses. It was only stamped out after the Edinburgh grave-robbers Burke and Hare turned to murder to supply their customers. London had its own Burke and Hare, as you will discover on the Strand walk, and the real Hare ended his days a beggar in St Giles, near Covent Garden (see page 87). Generally, the bodies supplied to St Thomas's – at a cost of 4 guineas, rising with demand to 14 guineas – were cut up in the dissecting room. But some may have found their way to the female operating theatre. This was built in 1821 in the attic of St Thomas's Chapel, next to the apothecary's herb garret. By a strange quirk of fate the theatre, complete with its wooden table and blood box, has survived and now forms part of the **Old Operating Theatre Museum and Herb Garret**.

Continue across Bedale Street. The Post Office building on the right was once the southern surgical wing of St Thomas's Hospital: female surgical patients were carried from their ward at the top of the building straight into the operating theatre in the church attic. Go under the railway bridge as far as the steps leading down to **Southwark Cathedral** (♨ right, in London Bridge station).

As you look ahead towards the start of present-day London Bridge, old London Bridge was a little to the right of this one, roughly where the leaning stone obelisk and **Southwark Information Centre** are now. For hundreds of years travellers approaching the bridge from this direction were invited to speculate on the dangers of resisting royal authority by the sight of the parboiled heads of traitors impaled on spikes atop the bridge's imposing gated entrance. Something almost equally horrific can be seen today if you walk a short distance past the information centre to the **London Dungeon**. Here you will find recreations of many of the more gory aspects of London's notorious past, including the murders of Jack the Ripper, featured in this book's East End chapter.

Now turn left down the steps and walk along the south side of Southwark Cathedral, once the priory church of St Mary Overie. As you pass the south porch, spare a thought for Thomas, 7th Baron Scales, whose naked body was dumped here one night in July 1460. Having defended the Tower of London against his Yorkist opponents in the Wars of the Roses, he had been allowed, when the garrison ran out of food, to leave the Tower and make his way to the sanctuary at Westminster. He was on his way there – by boat and at night because he was very unpopular with Londoners – when he was recognized by his boatmen and immediately killed.

Go through the gate into Cathedral Street and turn right. Ahead is (unsigned) Montague Close, once the priory of St Mary Overie and then the London home of Viscount Montague. Guy Fawkes, of Gunpowder Plot fame (see page 142), was once a servant in Montague's household and waited at table at the viscount's wedding in 1591.

Bear left along Cathedral Street to St Mary Overie dock and turn left into Pickford's Wharf. Ahead are the exposed remains of the great hall of Winchester House, the Bishop of Winchester's London house for five centuries, up to the 1640s. To the left, the building on the far side of Winchester Square stands on the approximate site of the original Clink, or at least the male part of it, which was in a courtyard slightly south of the palace's main living quarters.

Walk on past the palace ruins into Clink Street. On the left, where the street narrows, the Clink stood from 1745. In 1761 it was described as 'a very dismal hole', so it was probably no bad thing it was destroyed during the Gordon Riots of 1780 and never rebuilt. There is now a **Clink Prison Museum** on the site telling the story of 'naughty' Bankside and featuring, for those with a taste for a bit of punishment, 'restraining and torture devices (hands on)'.

Go under the railway bridge to Bank End. Here is the Anchor, a famous old riverside pub that stands on the site of the Castle, the first of the line of Bankside stews that stretched west along the river. From here you can see just how close they were to the bishop's residence at Winchester House.

Turn left and then right into Park Street, passing on the left the site of a once-famous brewery. Violent Austrian general Marshal Haynau, notorious for his cruelty towards Italian revolutionaries and Hungarians during the continental upheavals of 1848 and after, was visiting the brewery on 4 September 1850 when brewery workmen recognized him and set on him. Amid cries of 'Down with the Austrian butcher' he was chased into a pub and cornered before the police were able to rescue him. The same thing happened to him later in Brussels.

Further along Park Street, at No 123 (Old Theatre Court), is the preserved site of the Globe Theatre. Display panels tell you about its history and construction. The illustration in the one second from the left shows the Globe and the bear-baiting ring but they are the wrong way round: the Globe was where the bear ring is shown, and vice versa.

Carry on under the bridge. On the right, the **Rose Theatre Exhibition** features the exposed foundations of the old Rose Theatre, discovered during the building of this modern office block in 1989. The Rose was owned by Philip Henslowe, whose son-in-law, Edward Alleyn, was one of the top actors of the time. From 1594 Henslowe and Alleyn were also the main organizers of the bloody Bankside animal entertainments, and from 1604 they jointly held the post of Master of the Royal Bears, Bulls and Mastiff Dogs. In 1613, when the Globe burned down, they built the Hope Theatre/bear-baiting ring, just round the corner.

Beyond Rose Alley, turn right into Bear Gardens. In the little square was the last bear-baiting ring on Bankside, the one built after the Restoration in 1660 and subsequently visited by Pepys and Evelyn. As you walk down Bear Gardens you cross the site of the main ring in Shakespeare's time, opened around 1546 and rebuilt by Henslowe and Alleyn as the Hope.

At the end of Bear Gardens you come out in the middle of Bankside. Most of the stews were to the right, between where you are now and the Anchor, which you passed earlier. You can see how easy it would have been to get over here by boat from the City – but only during the day. During the night there was a curfew on the river, partly to prevent criminals escaping to Southwark under cover of darkness and partly to ensure that the stews stayed closed after sundown, according to the ancient rules enunciated in Henry II's time.

Turn left along Bankside. On the left now is the modern reconstruction of Shakespeare's Globe, as faithful a replica of a Tudor open-air playhouse as possible in the absence of a surviving original. The **Shakespeare's Globe Exhibition and Guided Tour** tells you all about Bankside as a theatre district in Shakespeare's time and also about the rivalry between the various forms of entertainment. Just beyond the new Globe is a small group of old houses on Cardinal's Wharf. Between them, narrow Cardinal Cap Alley – now gated at the wharf end and blocked at the other – was adjacent to the Cardinal's Hat stewhouse, the last one on Bankside. From here onward the riverside was mainly given over to commercial fish ponds (ironically, these were called stew ponds) until you got to Paris Garden, where dissipation resumed.

Ascend to the riverside walkway and walk along under the Millennium Bridge and past the Tate Modern. At the Founders Arms turn left through the arch by the Bankside Gallery into Hopton Street and turn right into a little square (**⚇** to right). You are now crossing the boundary between the liberties of the Clink and Paris Garden. Continue on along Hopton Street, effectively turning left. The entrance to Sampson House on the right (No 64) is roughly where the Swan Theatre stood. Behind it, underneath what is now the approach to Blackfriars Bridge, was the moated and fortified manor house of Paris Garden, where Baseley ran his gambling joint in Henry VIII's time. In 1603 a famous madam called Elizabeth Holland is said to have opened a high-class brothel here. Dinner with her 'queen of strumpets' Bell Broughton apparently cost the huge sum of £20, excluding any post-prandial entertainment. Mistress Holland's brothel flourished for some thirty years before being shut down in December 1631, following a short siege by the authorities. It is from this siege that it apparently got the curious name by which it is known to history, Holland's Leaguer.

Walk on down Hopton Street to Southwark Street and cross straight over into Bear Lane. At the end, turn right into Great Suffolk Street, go under three bridges and then, at the lights, turn left into Union Street. When you get to Ewer Street you are roughly opposite the site of the Monument Tavern, at 135 Union Street, where George Chapman, whom you encountered at the start of the walk, murdered his second known victim, barmaid Bessie Taylor, before moving to the Crown. Chapman's crimes are somehow compounded by the fact that he went through some form of marriage with all his known victims. Because of his obvious capacity for violence towards women and the fact that he knew Whitechapel well, some people have suggested he could have been Jack the Ripper, but his modus operandi was rather different.

Continue along Union Street and cross Southwark Bridge Road. On the right beyond Ayres Street note the old Ragged School and the plaque above its door which reads: 'The Mint and Gospel Lighthouse Mission Shaftesbury Society.' We come to the Mint shortly.

At the junction with Redcross Street, look ahead to the electricity substation on the left, built in the late 1990s to provide power for the Jubilee Line underground extension. Excavations during construction of the power station uncovered a mass of human bones which some have suggested could be the remains of Bankside prostitutes. These women were not allowed to be buried in the local churchyard of St Margaret's in Borough High Street, and instead were interred in what was called the Single Women's Churchyard, some distance from the parish church. However, since the remains found here appear to date from the 17th century at the earliest, it is unlikely that there is any specific connection between them and the medieval stews on Bankside. On the other hand, there could well be the bones of later prostitutes among them.

Turn right into Redcross Way. When this was called Redcross Street it was part of, or at least in the purlieus of, the Mint sanctuary. Jonathan Wild, the 18th century thief-taker and underworld boss (see page 39), is said to have stabled his horse at the Duke's Head pub in this street. Ahead now you can see the gaunt blocks of the Peabody Trust's Marshalsea Road Estate, which today covers much of the former Mint.

At the bottom of Redcross Way, cross Marshalsea Road into Mint Street (note Sanctuary Street to the left) and follow it round to the right. Ahead is Mint Street Park, where the local workhouse used to stand.

Mint Street was the centre of the Mint, one of the most notorious debtors' and criminals' sanctuaries in 17th century London. It grew up in the late 16th century after Brandon House, which had served as a royal mint for a few years on the 1540s, was demolished and built over. The place never had any legal status but it still took three Acts of Parliament to get rid of it. The last one, passed in 1723, worked only because it freed small debtors from arrest. On 16 July 1725 thousands of Minters finally departed the ghetto in a mass exodus that seemed to an eye-witness like one of the Jewish tribes going out of Egypt. The area stayed a slum, however, and gained a new notoriety in 1832 when London's first cholera epidemic broke out here.

Turn left into Weller Street. At the bottom cross Lant Street (where the 12-year-old Charles Dickens lodged while his parents were in the Marshalsea) into Toulmin Street, and then turn left into Webber Street. On the right now the Scovell housing estate covers the site of the second King's Bench Prison, opened in 1758 to replace the ancient one in Borough High Street. Webber Street was the northern boundary of the Rules of the King's Bench, an enormous area extending south to Elephant and Castle and west beyond St George's Circus, where the better-off prisoners paid for the privilege of living outside the prison walls. Several notorious characters who appear elsewhere in this book spent time in this King's Bench, including John Wilkes and Lord Cochrane (see pages 144 and 133 respectively). Wilkes's presence led to the St George's Fields Massacre on 10 May 1768, when soldiers opened fire on a mob of his supporters, killing several. Cochrane managed to escape in March 1815 by smuggling in a rope and climbing over the wall. Another notorious inmate was the conman and seducer John Hatfield, imprisoned for debt here in 1782. Having deserted two wives and children, Hatfield married a famous beauty from the Lake District in 1802. The publicity surrounding the union led to his exposure, and he was hanged for forgery less than a year afterwards.

From Webber Street, take the first right into Stones End Street, which marks the eastern end of the King's Bench. At the end turn left into Borough High Street and go straight over at the junction into Harper Road, formerly Horsemonger Lane. On your right now is the Inner London Sessions House, a courthouse first built here in the 1790s.

Further on is Newington Gardens, laid out over the site of the Horsemonger Lane Prison in the 1880s. Horsemonger Lane replaced the White Lion as the main county prison of Surrey and was built at the same time as the courthouse. It was here, on a scaffold erected on the roof so that spectators could see better, that Mr and Mrs Manning were hanged for the murder of their friend Patrick O'Connor in 1849. Charles Dickens watched the execution from a rented room in Bath Terrace on the far side of the gardens and was so horrified by the 'atrocious bearing, looks and language of the assembled spectators' that he wrote what later proved to be a highly influential letter to *The Times* calling for an end to public executions. The Mannings' tombstones are now in the **Cuming Museum**. The gaol was demolished in 1880 and replaced by a recreation ground which some elderly locals still refer to as the 'gaol playground'.

Turn left into Brockham Street and go left round Trinity Church Square. Turn left out of the square and then right into Swan Street. When you get to Great Dover Road, turn left on the main road to reach Borough station, where the walk ends.

Along the Fleet
Prisons and Executions

Before London was built up, several rivers could be seen flowing into the Thames in and around the old city. One of the most important was the Fleet. Rising in the Hampstead area, it flowed more or less due south through a relatively steep-sided valley into the Thames just west of the city wall. Farringdon Road, Farringdon Street and New Bridge Street were later built over it. Today, if you go down to Paul's Walk beneath Blackfriars Bridge at low tide and lean out over the parapet, you can see the gate through which the river emerges from its subterranean channel.

The Fleet is nowadays more a storm sewer than anything else. Before London got a purpose-built sewage system in the mid-19th century it, like other water-courses, was a sewer pure and simple. Lavatories – or 'houses of office' as they were quaintly called – were built out over it. The butchers of Newgate shambles cleansed the entrails of slaughtered beasts in it. Tanners washed their skins in it. And pig-keepers mucked out their sties into it.

As early as 1290 the 'putrid exhalations' rising out of the river not only swamped the smell of incense in neighbouring Whitefriars Monastery but killed several of the monks. In 1652 the river was still 'stinking and noisome'. In 1665, by which time the Fleet valley had been notorious for a century as the most unhealthy spot in London, more people died of the plague in parishes close to the Fleet than anywhere else in the capital.

After the 1666 Great Fire of London, which destroyed the picturesque but insanitary jumble of ancient buildings lining the river, an attempt was made to revive commercial traffic on the Fleet by making it into a canal and lining it with wharves. But the attempt failed, and by the early 18th century the poet Alexander Pope could still speak of the Fleet rolling its 'large tribute of dead dogs to the Thames'.

With the odd exception, most people with any sense or money stayed well clear of the Fleet valley. It was mainly the outcasts of society – the poor and the criminal – who populated the river's lower reaches. It was no coincidence that bordering the Fleet on the western outskirts of the city could be found pre-18th century London's main red-light district, its most notorious criminals' sanctuary, one of its three worst criminal rookeries, two of the capital's five main places of execution and no fewer than seven of its prisons. The brothel district, sanctuary and rookery appear on the walk. The introduction to this chapter focuses on prisons and places of execution, both of which helped make the Fleet district for centuries one of the most notorious parts of London.

Prisons

London today has five prisons, but before Victorian reforms it had at least three times that number. With the exception of the Tower of London, east of the City, and three institutions in Westminster – one of which was built in the 19th century – all were in a kind of Black Mile consisting of Borough High Street in Southwark, south of the river, and the Fleet valley, north of it.

If you have already read the previous chapter you will have encountered Southwark's five prisons: the Marshalsea, King's Bench, White Lion/Horsemonger Lane, Counter and Clink. Here in the environs of the Fleet valley you will find the sites of seven more. In geographical order, beginning at the mouth of the river, they were Bridewell, Ludgate, the Fleet, Newgate, Giltspur Street Compter, Clerkenwell House of Detention and Cold Bath Fields.

Many of these prisons contained large numbers of people whom we would not today regard as criminals at all – debtors. Imprisonment for debt started in the 14th century and became so common that several prisons – the Fleet, Marshalsea and King's Bench in particular – evolved into exclusive debtors' prisons while others – especially Newgate – had large areas set aside for debtors. Over the years, as many people were locked up for debt as for regular crimes.

Debtors spent far longer in prison than criminals, for whom custodial sentences did not replace transportation until well into the 19th century. In fact, it was not at all uncommon for debtors who never managed to pay off their debts to spend their whole lives in gaol. From the early 18th century onwards many of them had their families with them too, including the father of Charles Dickens (see page 16).

In general, London's prisons were lawless, brutal, corrupt places but, as always, if you were sufficiently well off you could buy a certain degree of comfort and protection. All the prisons had various classes of accommodation, with the best being suites of rooms in the keepers' own houses. The Fleet and the King's Bench even had areas (the Rules) outside the prison where debtors could live virtually normal lives, though they had to pay handsomely for the privilege.

If you did not have money, as most inmates did not, you were exposed to the full rigours of the system: violence, drunkenness, rape, disease (gaol fever, a kind of typhoid, periodically ravaged prisons, killing many more than the gallows ever did), hunger (eighty prisoners in the King's Bench starved to death in 1624), bitter cold in winter, stifling heat in summer (8–10 prisoners a *day* died in the Marshalsea during one particularly hot early-18th century summer) and, last but by no means least, the tyranny of the prison keepers.

Before central government took over the running of London's prisons in 1877, individual courts and jurisdictions administered them. In practice, most courts sold the right to run their prisons to so-called prison farmers. Prison farmers recouped their investment by charging prisoners exorbitant fees – at Newgate prisoners were charged a fee for having fetters put on, and then another for having them taken off again – and often subjected inmates to the most inhuman treatment.

One chronicler described Richard Imworth, an early keeper of the King's Bench, as a 'tormentor without pity'. Richard Husband, a 16th century keeper of a predecessor of the Giltspur Street Compter, was a 'wilful and headstrong man who dealt hard with the prisoners for his own advantage' – in fact, he was so bad that the Lord Mayor was forced to send him to Newgate, but he could not be sacked because prison keepers who had bought their prisons could be ousted only by a special Act of Parliament. Husband was soon back at his post, behaving just as cruelly as before and even letting thieves and prostitutes evade arrest by lodging in the prison for 4d a night. In the early 18th century the keeper of the Marshalsea tortured inmates with iron hoods, thumbscrews and beatings in order to extract their last pennies. He was also known to lock his charges up in small rooms with human corpses for company.

But the most notorious keeper of London's old gaols was attorney Thomas Bambridge, who with a partner bought the wardenship of the Fleet for £5000 in the early 18th century. He ruled the prison as his own private fiefdom, charging extortionate fees, keeping some prisoners in gaol long after they should have been released, allowing others to escape through a special exit door on payment of a substantial bribe, and stealing the money passers-by dropped into the poor prisoners' begging box set into the prison wall. On two occasions he was even tried for murdering a prisoner, but there was insufficient evidence to convict. Following a parliamentary investigation in 1729, which concluded that he had been guilty of 'the most notorious breaches of his trust, great extortions, and the highest crimes and misdemeanours', a special Act of Parliament was passed and he was dispossessed of his private theatre of cruelty. Twenty years later he committed suicide. No wonder.

Executions

At one time murderers and other felons were executed in public all over London, often – especially in the more sensational cases – at the scenes of their crimes. 18th century murderess Sarah Malcolm suffered in this way, as you will discover during this chapter's walk.

From early times certain places became particularly notorious as execution sites. These included Kennington Common in South London, where Surrey criminals were hanged, and Execution Dock in Wapping, the favoured spot for executing pirates and sea-rovers. But the main places of execution were the Tower of London, for the high-ranking, and Smithfield followed by Tyburn and Newgate for the less exalted. The Tower and Tyburn feature respectively on the City and Mayfair/St James's walks (see pages 49 and 134); Smithfield and Newgate are included in this chapter's walk.

Being a fortress and Britain's main state prison, the Tower of London was particularly associated with the execution of traitors and other state prisoners. Tower executions took place both inside the Tower – on Tower Green – and outside it, on Tower Hill. Historically, Tower Green was favoured for executions which needed to be swift and private. For example, two of Henry VIII's wives, Anne Boleyn and Catherine Howard, were beheaded here in the 16th century. Most of Tower Green's victims were of high rank, but the last ones were actually three ordinary soldiers who had taken part in a peaceful mutiny in 1743.

Public executions designed as judicial spectacles were held outside the Tower on Tower Hill. This became the traditional spot for executing those of high social or military rank, with the method being beheading rather than common hanging. In 1745 the Jacobite Lord Lovat was beheaded on Tower Hill. Just before he laid his head on the block a grandstand collapsed, killing 12 people, an event which is said to have afforded the aged peer a certain grisly satisfaction. After Lovat's death, beheading was no longer practised, so Tower Hill consequently lost much of its social cachet. The last executions there were in 1780 when a sailor and two prostitutes were hanged for their part in the Gordon Riots, a week-long orgy of violence during which London was almost completely in the grip of the mob.

In medieval times, the main place for executing ordinary criminals was a grove of elm trees at Smithfield, an open space and fairground just outside the City wall. During the era of religious persecution in the 16th century, Smithfield was also the scene of numerous burnings of heretics and other religious dissidents, especially the Reformation's Protestant martyrs, commemorated today in nearby Clerkenwell Church. Queen Mary burnt 49 Protestants at Smithfield in her short reign (1553–8), seven in one day. In 1849 labourers digging a sewer unearthed what appeared to be the remains of the site of the fire, including a charred stake with a staple and ring attached to it. In at least one case a man was boiled to death at Smithfield; this was Richard Rose, convicted in the 1530s of poisoning 17 people and attempting to poison his master, the Bishop of Lancaster. It is said that after the fire beneath the cauldron was lit it took two hours for him to die.

In the late 1300s Tyburn, then a couple of miles west of London, succeeded Smithfield as London's main place of execution. During the next four centuries it was probably the most notorious spot in London, surpassing even the Tower in horror and fascination. Most of its 60,000 victims died on the infamous triple tree, London's first permanent gallows. Erected in 1571, the tree consisted of three posts 18ft (5.5m) high connected by crossbeams 9ft (2.75m) long, with each beam capable of holding eight people. Although only one occasion is recorded when the triple tree bore its full complement of 24, multiple executions were the rule rather than the exception.

Most Tyburn victims were sentenced at the Old Bailey, the main courthouse for London and the county of Middlesex. They spent their last days in the condemned hold in neighbouring Newgate, the main prison for the same places. Designed to deter, executions were public spectacles from beginning to end. People were allowed (on payment of a fee, of course) into Newgate to ogle the condemned in the hold. On the day before execution the public were also permitted to attend a special service in the prison chapel when the condemned sat around a coffin in a railed enclosure, listening to an edifying sermon. The execution day itself was a public holiday, with tens of thousands turning out to watch the procession of prisoners as it wound its way slowly along the nearly three miles (5km) of road between Newgate and Tyburn. The prisoners were allowed a last, free, drink at a pub at St Giles-in-the-Fields (see page 86), the routine joke being that they would pay for it on the way back. At Tyburn spectators watched from the grandstand, known after its owner as Mother Proctor's Pews, or from lamplighters' ladders leaned together to make a kind of step-ladder. Those who couldn't afford a special vantage point milled about eating gingerbread and oranges and waiting for the 'turning off'.

It was called 'turning off' because in the early days the prisoners had to climb a ladder to the noose; if they did not then have the nerve to jump off themselves the hangman had to twist the ladder to dislodge them. Later they stood in the back of a cart which was drawn away from under them. They died of strangulation rather than, as in later times, a broken neck; it was thus common for family and friends to pull on the victim's legs to hasten death. Earl Ferrers, executed in 1760 for murdering his steward, was apparently the first man to be hung over a trapdoor.

Eventually the almost day-long Tyburn carnival became too obscene even for hardened 18th century sensibilities, so from December 1783 executions were held at Newgate. The move certainly brought an end to the grisly procession through St Giles and along what is now Oxford Street, but, with huge crowds packed into the relatively confined space in front of Newgate, spectators faced the very real danger of death from crowd panics and stampedes. Nearly a hundred people were killed or seriously injured at the hanging of Haggerty and Holloway in 1807 (see page 87), and in 1831 three people were trampled to death at the execution of bodysnatchers John Bishop and Thomas Williams (see page 99).

Tragedies like this were averted only when public executions were stopped. The last man to be hanged in public in London was Irishman Michael Barrett, executed outside Newgate in May 1868 for his part in the Fenian bomb attack on Clerkenwell prison (see page 37). Thereafter executions took place inside Newgate until 1902, when the ancient prison was finally closed.

THE FLEET VALLEY WALK

Start and finish: Blackfriars underground station (Circle and District lines).
Length: 3 miles (5km).
Refreshments: Plenty of places in Fleet Street, near the start of the walk, and around Farringdon station, about two-thirds of the way round, but Exmouth Market at the halfway stage (many new restaurants, bars and cafés) and Clerkenwell Green soon after (attractive square with seats and shade) are the natural places to stop.
Route note: If you do this walk at the weekend, you miss a short section near the beginning which goes through the Inner Temple. Follow the dotted line on the map to pick up the walk again a little later on in Fleet Street.

From Blackfriars station, subway exit 8 brings you out on the west side of New Bridge Street, facing north up the valley of the Fleet. It was on scaffolding under Blackfriars Bridge behind you that Italian banker Roberto Calvi was found hanging on 18 June 1982, his wallet stuffed with cash and his pockets with bricks. No one has yet been convicted of his murder, but the theory is that he was killed by the Sicilian Mafia because he lost money borrowed from them to cover debts of the failed Banco Ambrosiano, of which he was chairman. The Mafia subsequently recovered its money, but Calvi was made to pay for his financial ineptitude nonetheless.

Continue along New Bridge Street, walking away from the bridge and crossing the entrance to Tudor Street. No 14 New Bridge Street, on the left, is the former entrance to Bridewell prison, the earliest of the so-called Houses of

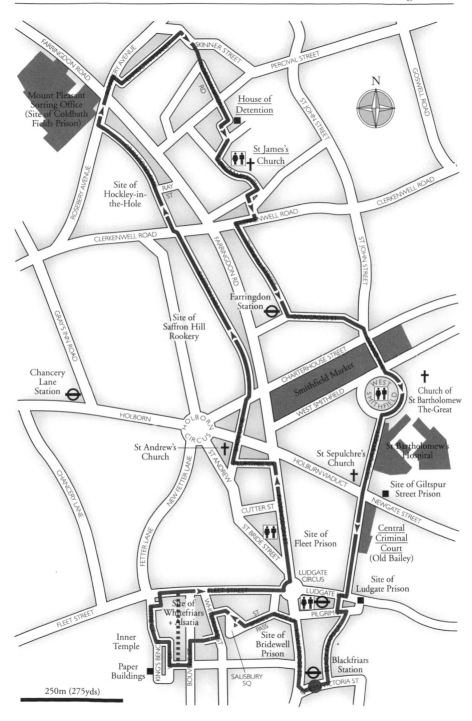

250m (275yds)

Correction where strumpets, vagrants and other petty offenders were whipped and put to work in an attempt to cure them of their disorderly ways. By the early 1700s the public whippings of semi-naked prostitutes in a black-draped room had become such a popular sight for men about town that a special balustraded gallery had to be built to accommodate them. The whippings were stopped later in the century, and after three centuries the prison closed in 1855.

Cross Bridewell Place, the northern limit of the prison, and turn next left into Bride Lane. When this bends round to the right, go straight on into St Bride's Passage and up the steps. The height gained represents the west bank of the Fleet river. Go straight on through the covered walkway into Salisbury Square, cross diagonally right to the covered entrance to Hanging Sword Alley, and follow the alley round to the left. This area was well known for its fencing schools during the 17th century, when men commonly wore swords. In the 18th century Hanging Sword Alley was home to a notorious criminals' drinking den called Blood Bowl House. Artist William Hogarth used it as one of the locations in his pictorial story of the Idle Apprentice, a young lad who ends his days on the gallows.

At the end of the alley, turn left into Whitefriars Street, formerly called Water Lane. Until the 1870s there was an old inn on the right where, a century earlier (on Wednesday 12 January 1763 to be precise), the 22-year-old James Boswell, later the biographer of Dr Johnson, successfully bedded actress Louisa Lewis after a month-long siege. It was the first sex Boswell had had since arriving in London two months previously, and he was mighty proud of his 'god-like' performance, climaxing no fewer than five times. Louisa was apparently satisfied after two. 'I surely may be styled a Man of Pleasure,' the would-be rake confided proudly to his diary after his night of lust.

When you draw abreast of the Harrow pub on the left, turn right into Ashentree Court. You are now entering what were once the precincts of the Carmelite or Whitefriars Monastery. At the end of Ashentree Court, in the basement of the modern office block on the right, you can see the little medieval vault which is the only surviving part of the monastery. After its closure in the mid-16th century the monastery was mostly built over, but its medieval right of sanctuary remained. Strictly speaking the sanctuary was for debtors only, but thieves, murderers, prostitutes and others took advantage of it to create a lawless and violent no-go area where officers of the law feared to tread. Called Alsatia – after Alsace, the disputed borderland between Germany and France where fighting was more or less constant – it was the most notorious of several similar sanctuaries in 17th century London. The Mint in Southwark was another (see page 23).

From the medieval vault continue on through Magpie Alley to Bouverie Street, turn left and then at Tudor Street turn right. Ahead you

Plate 1: *The modern-day Anchor pub stands on the site of the Castle, one of medieval Southwark's notorious stewhouses, or brothels (see pages 12 and 21).*

Plate 2: *This Southwark house is connected with a Victorian murder (see page 18).*

Plate 3: *Inside one of Tudor Southwark's animal baiting theatres (see page 13).*

Plate 4: *Underneath the arches of Blackfriars bridge. Italian banker Roberto Calvi was found hanging here on 18 June 1982 (see page 30).*

Plate 5: *This old print shows the bull- and bear-baiting rings at Southwark, and, in the centre, the notorious Holland's Leaguer brothel in Paris Garden (see page 22).*

Plate 6: *Clerkenwell's House of Detention musuem incorporates cells from an old prison (see page 37).*

Plate 7: *Newgate, once London's most notorious prison, burns during the Gordon Riots of 1780. The Old Bailey now stands on the site (see pages 26 and 38).*

Plate 8: *Robbing graveyards for corpses and selling them to medical schools for dissection was big business in early 19th-century London (see page 19).*

Plate 9: *Pickpockets were always active at Smithfield's St Bartholomew's Fair (see page 37).*

FATHER THAMES INTRODUCING HIS OFFSPRING TO THE FAIR CITY OF LONDON.

DIPHTHERIA.   SCROFULA.   CHOLERA.

Plate 10: *The Fleet and other rivers in London were once little better than open sewers. By the 19th century the Thames was a major source of disease in the capital (see page 25).*

can now see a gateway leading into the Inner Temple, one of the four inns of court where barristers have their chambers. When Alsatia was in full swing, gates in the Temple wall connecting the two enclaves led to frequent battles between the lawyers and their troublesome neighbours. In July 1691 the lawyers walled this particular gate up, but the Alsatians objected and knocked it down. A fierce fight ensued in which two people were killed and several wounded. 'Captain' Francis White, the Alsatians' ringleader, was convicted of murder and hanged in nearby Fleet Street in 1693. Four years later an Act of Parliament was passed which eventually led to the final suppression of the sanctuaries.

At the end of Tudor Street carry on through the gate into the Temple. (If it is a weekend and the gate is closed, pick up the walk again by turning right into Temple Lane and making your way via Lombard Lane – one of the main streets of Alsatia – and Pleydell Court into Fleet Street.) Straight ahead is Paper Buildings. Years after his ignominious dismissal from the Fleet prison, its sadistic warden Bambridge cut his throat in his chambers at 9 Paper Buildings on 11 July 1741.

Turn right now into King's Bench Walk. Bearing left towards the top you pass the Temple library and an archway leading into another part of the Temple called – before it was bombed during World War II – Tanfield Court. A young barrister living here in February 1733 found certain strange items in his rooms which it turned out his cleaner, 22-year-old Sarah Malcolm, had stolen from another of her employers, one Mrs Duncomb. During the robbery, the elderly Mrs Duncomb and two of her female servants had been murdered. Sarah admitted the robbery but denied the murders, but went to the gallows anyway. Huge crowds turned out to see her hanged in Fleet Street, just outside Temple Gate. So closely were the spectators packed together that a local woman was able to cross the road by walking on their shoulders.

Continue to the top of King's Bench Walk, and then go through the arch in Mitre Court Buildings into Old Mitre Court, passing, on the right, Serjeant's Inn, another lawyers' enclave. Just before you go through a further arch, leading into Fleet Street, turn right and then left into a little alley in the corner called Hare Place. This is all that remains of a once much longer passage called Ram Alley, which stretched back from Fleet Street to King's Bench Walk. Ram Alley was probably the most notorious thoroughfare in all Alsatia. Overhanging houses nearly met at the top, making it dark and noisome. The footway was little more than a sewer, and every house that was not a cookshop for a neighbouring inn was a brothel or an unlicensed drinking den.

As you emerge from Hare Place onto Fleet Street you are close to where Sarah Malcolm and 'Captain' White were hanged. You are also close to the site of another particularly notorious 18th century murder. This took place in Fleur-de-Lis Court, which ran off the north side of Fleet Street until 1984, when Fetter Lane, to your left, was widened. In 1767 servant girl Mary Clifford died here of injuries received from her sadistic employer, midwife Elizabeth Brownrigg. Mrs Brownrigg was hanged at Tyburn in September that year. Her death mask is in Scotland Yard's crime museum.

Turn right down Fleet Street (picking up the weekend detour at covered Pleydell Court). When you get to Bouverie Street you are standing outside the main gate of Whitefriars. Another street execution took place here in 1612, when the two assassins of Whitefriars fencing master John Turner were hanged, one 6ft (2m) higher than the other because he was of higher social rank! They had been hired for the job by Scottish peer Lord Sanquhar, who had lost an eye in a fencing match with Turner five years previously and somewhat belatedly sought his revenge. Sanquhar also went to the gallows for the crime, but outside Westminster Hall, which you pass on the Westminster walk (see page 142).

At the lights just ahead, cross Fleet Street and continue on down the hill. When you get to the flamboyant Art Deco office building with the clock on the front, note the gateway at the far end marked 'in', just before No 133. This marks the approximate site of the house where Mary Frith lived and where she died on 26 July 1659, aged 78. By rights she should have been hanged long before because ever since her youth in Shakespeare's London she had been a notorious thief, pickpocket, highwayman and fence, usually dressing in men's clothes and much given to roistering and drinking. When she was about 30 Middleton and Dekker immortalized her in their play *The Roaring Girl* (1611) under the name by which she is best known today – Moll Cutpurse. Moll was buried in the churchyard of St Bride's across the road.

Carry on down Fleet Street to Ludgate Circus and turn left into Farringdon Street. Over on the right (effectively on the other side of the Fleet) the big office block (Caroone House, No 14) stands on the site of the Fleet prison. Apart from the Tower, Newgate and the Fleet were the oldest prisons in London, having been founded in the 1100s. Originally the Fleet was moated, which cannot have done much for the health of its inmates. Later a 40ft (12m) wall ensured security. Until it evolved into a debtors' prison, it received prisoners from various courts, including the Court of Common Pleas, which administered it, and the infamous Court of Star Chamber, which, until its abolition in the 17th century, had the power to lock people up without trial. In the 1740s John Cleland was in the Fleet when he wrote what must be the most famous pornographic novel in the English language – *Fanny Hill* (1750).

The Liberty of the Fleet (or Rules) extended left and right of the prison and also up the hill behind it to the Old Bailey. Here in the 17th and 18th centuries so-called Fleet parsons – drunken, indebted and otherwise 'fallen' clergymen – married people in taverns without banns or licences, for, of course, the appropriate fee. Fleet marriages were legal but led to so many abuses – bigamy, for example, and the forced marriages of heiresses to fortune-hunting scoundrels – that they were abolished by the Marriage Act of 1754. Thereafter people who wished to marry secretly or in haste had to cross the border into Scotland – hence the fame of Gretna Green.

The north side of Fleet prison was bounded by Fleet Lane, the same as today's Old Fleet Lane, on the north side of Caroone House. In the 17th century this was a notorious haunt of prostitutes, many of whom no doubt earned good money from frustrated debtors in the adjacent gaol. Prostitutes were regularly admitted to London's old prisons, and on one occasion in Shakespeare's time the managers of Bridewell were even found to be running it as a brothel. In July 1664 a particularly attractive Fleet Lane whore caught the attention of Samuel Pepys. He became so obsessed with her that he came back on several occasions just to get a glimpse of her. But he never actually went to bed with her.

Now continue along Farringdon Street, following the course of the Fleet river. The height of the bridge ahead, built in the 19th century to carry a new road from Holborn to the City, gives you some idea of the depth of the river valley here. Just before the bridge, turn left into Plumtree Court and then right into Shoe Lane, and continue under the bridge. Beyond the bridge, this part of Shoe Lane used to be called Field Lane. Leading as it did to the notorious thieves' rookery of Saffron Hill, the lane had an evil reputation. In the early 18th century it was the address of London's biggest male brothel, Mother Clap's molly house ('molly' was slang for homosexual). In those days sodomy was a capital offence: after a raid in February 1726, three patrons were hanged at Tyburn. By Dickens's time the place had become a 'celebrated receptacle for stolen goods'; people said you could have your handkerchief stolen at one end of the street and buy it back at the other!

When you get to Charterhouse Street you are standing at the beginning of Chick Lane, another notorious street, which ran down to the Fleet on your right and then up the hill on the far side to the sheep pens in West Smithfield, roughly where the green-domed Smithfield Market is now. An ancient house down by the river was supposed to have been a regular rendezvous of Jonathan Wild and highwayman Jack Sheppard. It was full of hidden doors and secret hiding places, and there was a plank bridge at the back so that inmates could escape across the Fleet. It was pulled down in 1840, some fifteen years before the whole area was cleared for the Clerkenwell improvements of the mid-1850s.

From Shoe Lane, cross Charterhouse Street diagonally right and go down the steps into Saffron Hill. Walk along for some distance, crossing Greville Street. By the mid-19th -century this area had degenerated into one of the three worst slum rookeries in Victorian London — St Giles near Covent Garden (see page 79) and Bermondsey in East London being the others. Even the local vicar from nearby St Andrew's Holborn dared not visit without a police escort. Dickens lived under a mile away while writing *Oliver Twist* (1837–9) and located Fagin's lair in it. 'A dirtier or more wretched place he had never seen' is Oliver's reaction when he first sets eyes on Saffron Hill. It was narrow, smelly and muddy, full of empty shops, busy pubs, screaming children and drunken, brawling people. Some of these would have been Italians, for it was at about this time that immigrants from the Mediterranean — some of them beggar-masters with troops of professional boy beggars — were beginning to turn the Holborn/Clerkenwell area into London's Italian quarter.

Just beyond St Cross Street you come to Saffron Street, on the right. Near here in 1865 an incident in a pub led to a fight between locals and Italian immigrants and very nearly to a tragic miscarriage of justice. One local was killed in the fight and Serafino Pelizzioni was sentenced to death for his murder. But it was found at the last moment that he had been wrongly accused. His cousin was subsequently imprisoned for manslaughter.

Continue to the end of Saffron Hill, cross Clerkenwell Road and go down Herbal Hill to Ray Street, originally known — because of its low-lying position — as Hockley-in-the-Hole. Around 1700, when Hockley-in-the-Hole was on the northern edge of London, Bankside's violent sports, which by then had lost favour with the upper classes, were transferred here for the entertainment of the local riff-raff, mainly butchers who liked to see a bit of blood — human or animal, it was all the same to them. The Coach and Horses pub to your left is said to stand on the site of the ring where the dogfights, and bull- and bear-baiting and prize fights between swordsmen were held.

Cross Ray Street into Crawford Passage. At the end, cross Bakers Row, go past the trees into the remains of Cold Bath Square and continue on to Rosebery Avenue. Across the road, Mount Pleasant sorting office stands on the site of Cold Bath Fields Prison, built on a public dungheap in 1794 and closed in 1877. This aptly named institution soon became notorious for its punishing regime of solitary confinement and arduous treadwheeling. The latter was so hard that the Royal Artillery stopped sending its offenders here because they returned unfit for service! London's criminals were unused to the treatment they encountered at Cold Bath Fields and nicknamed the gaol the Bastille, usually shortened to Steel.

Turn right past the fire station and cross Farringdon Road into Exmouth Market. At the end, turn right into Rosoman Street and, when the road bends left, carry straight on, joining up with Northampton Road. Carry on along here as far as Corporation Row. Behind the wall, Kingsway College stands on the site of an old prison known as the Clerkenwell House of Detention, dating from the early 17th century and closed in 1877. In 1724 notorious highwayman Jack Sheppard escaped from the prison by scaling the 22ft (6.7m) wall with his fat mistress Edgeworth Bess on his back. In 1867 Irish Fenians, forerunners of the IRA, blew a hole in the prison's north wall in a bid to free two colleagues. The attempt failed, but the explosion wrecked many of the houses which then stood in Corporation Row; six people, including two children, were killed instantly, nine died later and about forty were injured or disabled for life. Some of the original cells of the prison now form part of the **House of Detention** museum (entrance straight ahead).

From the entrance to Corporation Row, go slightly right into Clerkenwell Close and follow this road round to the left, past the entrance to **St James's Church** (⛪), which has a memorial to the Fenians' victims. Clerkenwell Close brings you to Clerkenwell Green. This was occasionally used as a place of execution. In 1538, for example, 20,000 Londoners saw three men, including one of the city's hangmen, hanged for robbery at Smithfield's St Bartholomew's Fair.

Turn right now, and then left in front of the old Middlesex Sessions House. At Clerkenwell Road, go right and then first left into Turnmill Street, an ancient thoroughfare which ran along the east side of the Fleet river. Turnmill Street was already known for its whores in the 15th century. By the time of Shakespeare (who has Justice Shallow in *Henry IV Part II* boasting about sowing his wild oats in Turnmill Street) it had become London's main red-light district north of the river. Court records reveal at least five brothels in the street between 1613 and 1616.

At the end, turn left into Cowcross Street. Follow this round to Charterhouse Street and cross over into Grand Avenue, which takes you through Smithfield Meat Market into West Smithfield. Keep left round the square. In the corner you come to the west entrance of St Bartholomew's Church. The victims of Smithfield burnings had to face this entrance, so the executions must have taken place very near here. Ahead of you, on the wall of St Bartholomew's Hospital, is a memorial to Sir William Wallace, the Scottish patriot hung, drawn and quartered at Smithfield on 23 August 1305. Not all executions here were official. In 1754 two thief-takers called Egan and Salmon, pilloried at Smithfield for luring young men into crime and then betraying them to gain the rewards, were actually stoned to death by a crowd outraged that the two principals should have escaped the death sentence when several of their victims had gone to the gallows.

Turn left out of West Smithfield into Giltspur Street. Cock Lane, on the right, was one of the few places in the Middle Ages where prostitutes were legally allowed to ply their trade. In 1762 the notorious Cock Lane Ghost hoax was perpetrated at a house about halfway down on the left-hand side. Well known people including the Duke of York and Dr Johnson came to investigate, but it turned out that the noises supposedly made by the ghost – said to be the spirit of a young woman poisoned with arsenic – were in fact the product of a young girl scratching and knocking on a board concealed beneath her stays. Note the inscription on the right-hand corner of the entrance to the street, with its references to resurrection men. Although it is questionable that the Fortune of War pub which once stood here was in fact the main port of call for bodysnatchers north of the river (if indeed there ever was such a place), two notorious snatchers called Bishop and Williams, who you will meet again on the Strand walk (see page 99), certainly used it as a rendezvous.

At the end of Giltspur Street is St Sepulchre's Church. Murderess Sarah Malcolm, whom you encountered at the start of this walk, was briefly interred here after her execution. Later her skeleton was exhumed and sent to the Botanical Garden at Cambridge, whence it has since disappeared. Opposite St Sepulchre's, the Merrill Lynch building stands on the site of the Giltspur Street prison, opened in 1791 and closed in 1855. One of the two prisons belonging to the sheriffs of London, this was the third and last incarnation of a medieval prison which originally stood in Bread Street. Richard Husband, featured in this chapter's introduction as one of London's notorious prison keepers, ran the Bread Street prison during the 16th century.

Cross Newgate Street into Old Bailey. On the left-hand corner the Central Criminal Court, better known as the Old Bailey, stands on the site of Newgate Prison, closed in 1902. In this broad open space thousands gathered to watch public executions outside Newgate from 1783 until 1868. The better-off folk rented rooms in houses and pubs opposite, like the Magpie and Stump, which survives in modern form. The hoi-polloi thronged the street, risking death in the crush. The gallows were erected outside the debtors' door, which was approximately where the disused gated entrance to the **Central Criminal Court** is now. Many characters in this book breathed their last on this gallows. The gaol was to the left of where you are standing (the original gaol was in the gatehouse straddling Newgate) and the sessions house was to the right. In between was the infamous Press Yard, off which was the Press Room where murderers and others who refused to plead were 'pressed' with increasingly heavy weights until they either agreed to plead or, in a few cases, died. On the prison side was the executioner's kitchen, where the heads and limbs of dismembered traitors would be boiled in bay salt and cumin seed to preserve them when they were impaled on spikes fixed to the top of London's various gates, especially the one at the south end of London Bridge. It was not unknown for the executioner and inmates to chuck the heads about like a football. In 1820 the last beheadings in England took place outside Newgate when, for a fee of 20 guineas, a masked resurrection man armed with an amputating knife cut off the heads of five men who had just been hanged for their part in the Cato Street conspiracy (see page 132).

Just beyond the Old Bailey sessions house – where the modern court extension is now – stood Surgeons' Hall, the headquarters of what later became the Royal College of Surgeons. Here from 1752 onwards were brought the corpses of executed murderers, either for public dissection on the premises or for clearance for dissection at one of the teaching hospitals. Like street execution, dissection was regarded as an especial humiliation. Lord Ferrers, hanged at Tyburn for murdering his steward (see page 29), not surprisingly felt the insult particularly acutely; his body was delivered to Surgeons' Hall in his own coach on 5 May 1760. It was in the late 18th century, when the supply of bodies from Surgeons' Hall proved inadequate to meet the increasing demands of the expanding surgical profession, that resurrection men began digging up corpses from graveyards and selling them to the hospitals. London's most notorious gang of bodysnatchers operated in Southwark (see page 19).

Carry on down Old Bailey. On the right No 30 (the middle one of a parade of modern shops) stands approximately on the site of Jonathan Wild's 'Office for the Recovery of Lost and Stolen Property', deliberately positioned close to Newgate and the Old Bailey. In the early 18th century Wild earned himself the title of Thief-Taker General for his success at recovering stolen goods and securing the conviction and execution of criminals, for both of which he was rewarded under the official thief-taking system. In reality he was the biggest gangster of them all, achieving his success by controlling the very criminals who carried out the crimes which he purported to solve. In 1725 this criminal mastermind – perhaps the greatest London has ever known – himself went to the gallows for his part in handling stolen lace worth just £10. His skeleton survives in the Royal College of Surgeons in Lincoln's Inn Fields.

At the end of Old Bailey you come to Ludgate Hill. Just to your left stood Ludgate itself, used from early times, like Newgate, as a gaol. Ludgate was a debtors' gaol for relatively high-status freemen of the City of London, and as such was more comfortable than other London prisons. But inmates were still mulcted for every last penny and, if a harsh keeper was in charge, badly treated as well. The gate was removed in 1760, but the prison lived on as the Ludgate wing of various other prisons, latterly Whitecross Street, closed in 1870.

Cross straight over Ludgate Hill into Pageantmaster Court. Turn left into Pilgrim Street and right into Ludgate Broadway, and carry on into Black Friars Lane. Follow this all the way down the hill until you come to Blackfriars station, where the walk ends.

The City
Frauds and Swindles

London began life as the City of London, the famous square mile east of Fleet Street, with the Tower of London at one end and St Paul's at the other.

As the space between London and Westminster filled up, the old City of London developed into the new metropolis's business district, known as just the City. Then, in the 19th century, as Britain industrialized and her worldwide colonial and commercial empires grew, the City started to specialize in one particular aspect of business – finance. If there is a single key date in this transformation it is probably 1811, when industrial shares were first quoted on the London Stock Exchange.

By the mid-19th century Britain had an increasingly large middle class looking for somewhere to put its money. It also had an almost completely unregulated financial system. The inevitable result of this dangerous combination of circumstances was a series of spectacular frauds, swindles and crashes. These made the City in Victorian times notorious in a way it hadn't been since the South Sea Bubble of 1720 and was not to be again until the yuppie era of the 1980s, when deregulation and takeover mania once again generated a healthy crop of financial scandals and melt-downs.

During this jungle era of the City – which lasted roughly from the 1850s through to the 1920s – the newspapers were full of accounts of business frauds large and small. The biggest ones provided inspiration for novelists like Dickens and Trollope, playwrights like Granville Barker and W.S. Gilbert and artists like William Frith, who painted a Hogarth-like series of pictures called *The Road to Wealth* that began with the financier in his office and ended with him as a prisoner in Westminster's Millbank prison (where the Tate Britain gallery now is).

Allowing for some chronological licence, Frith's model could have been any one of a handful of notorious fraudsters who were major public figures in their day and who have since gone down in history as some of the biggest rogues of all time. There was John Sadleir, for example, the banker who ruined just about the whole of County Tipperary in Ireland; Albert Grant, the so-called Baron who sold shares in mines that probably never existed and built one of the biggest houses in London on the proceeds; and Whitaker Wright, the archetypal Victorian company promoter who swallowed a capsule of cyanide rather than face the disgrace of prison.

The stories of these and other fraudulent financiers form the introduction to this chapter. On the walk that follows you will pass some of the sites associated with their nefarious operations as well as locations connected with other notorious people and events in the City's long and not always respectable history.

John Sadleir

John Sadleir was an ambitious Irishman from County Tipperary. His family owned and ran the Tipperary Bank; he himself was bred as a solicitor. After practising for a while in Dublin, he came to England in 1846. At the time the country was in the grip of railway mania. Ostensibly Sadleir was agent for a number of Irish railway companies, but his real agenda was to make his own name and fortune. Success came with amazing rapidity. Within two years he was a Member of Parliament and chairman of a prestigious City bank, the London and County, based at 21 Lombard Street. Within four years he was hailed as one of the richest men in London. The trappings of wealth included a town house at 11 Gloucester Square, near Hyde Park, and a country house (with stud) at Leighton Buzzard in Bedfordshire. In 1853 his star rose even higher when he was appointed a Treasury minister – albeit a junior one – in Lord Aberdeen's Conservative government.

But, just as the future seemed so rosy for Sadleir, the tide began to turn. His first mistake was to abuse his position at the Treasury for his own private financial gain. His second mistake was to be found out. Having been forced to resign from the government, he was also soon squeezed out of the London and County. Now his whole edifice, built on nothing more secure than confidence, began to collapse.

The end came on Saturday 16 February 1856 when he was obliged, but unable, to pay for some shares. Sadleir could not face the disgrace of ruin. He went to his club, wrote two suicide notes (see page 126), went home and had dinner, and then, after midnight, made his way from Gloucester Square to Hampstead Heath. Here he poured some prussic acid into a silver cream jug and drank it off. His body was found the next morning about 150 yards from Jack Straw's Castle, a pub still very much in existence at the high point of the Heath.

It later transpired that during his brief but meteoric career Sadleir had forged, swindled and stolen his way through £750,000, a phenomenal sum for the time. £150,000 of this had come from forged shares in the Royal Swedish Railway, another company he chaired. A further slice came from the sale of land in Ireland to which he had forged the title deeds. But the biggest single amount – some £200,000 – was what he had obtained by fair means or foul from his own family bank. His embezzlements broke the bank, and the bank's failure in turn ruined hundreds of small investors in Tipperary – tradesmen, farmers, merchants and the like.

So resounding was Sadleir's crash and so awful were the results of his gigantic swindles that Charles Dickens was moved to immortalize him in the character of Merdle in *Little Dorrit* (1855–7). In the novel, Merdle, having been the greatest financier of his age, is exposed as 'the greatest forger and the greatest thief that ever cheated the gallows' before slitting his own throat with a penknife.

Jabez Balfour

In 1868 25-year-old Jabez Balfour founded the Liberator Permanent Benefit Building Society. It was to be neither liberating, permanent nor of benefit to anyone save J. Balfour.

No doubt he started out with the best of intentions. His aims were to encourage thrift and to enable working people with nonconformist, temperance backgrounds like his own to buy their own homes. The simple message struck a chord with savers, and thousands sent in their deposits. After just eleven years the Liberator had taken in over £1m and become the largest building society in the country.

Liberator investors reasonably assumed that their money was being lent out on mortgage, with any surplus being safely tucked away in gilt-edged securities. But somewhere along the line Balfour had strayed from the path of rectitude. He was using the Liberator's money to fund his own wealthy lifestyle (large house in Croydon and country estate in Oxfordshire), his political ambitions (Member of Parliament in 1880 and Mayor of Croydon in 1883) and, worst of all, his property speculations.

Quite early on Balfour had realized that he could make more profit by lending money to builders than by funding long-term mortgages. Hundreds of thousands of Liberator pounds were diverted into the business of Croydon builder and personal friend J.W. Hobbs. When Hobbs's business looked like going under, Balfour took it over and became a property developer himself, with a group of companies including a new bank, the London and General, based alongside the Liberator at 20 Budge Row in the City.

Using Liberator funds, Balfour became one of the biggest property developers in London, building apartment blocks, hotels and clubs in the centre of the city and housing estates in the suburbs. But these speculations failed to generate sufficient return, and so there came a point when, even though the Liberator was continuing to attract hundreds of thousands of pounds in new deposits every year, there wasn't enough coming in to pay what needed to go out – in particular, interest on earlier deposits. That point was reached on 2 September 1892, when the London and General, quickly followed by the Liberator, crashed. In the fallout it emerged that, of the £3.5m lent out by the Liberator, 93% had gone to Balfour. Only a measly 1.2% had been lent out on mortgage to society members.

Balfour fled to South America but after a couple of years was brought back, convicted and sentenced to 14 years in prison. Meanwhile, so many people had been reduced to penury by his swindle that a special relief fund had to be set up, with a royal prince at the head of it. The fund continued for over twenty years, raising £156,000 and helping more than 3000 individuals, mostly elderly widows and spinsters who had been relying on Balfour and the Liberator to save them from the workhouse. Despite its noble name, the Liberator had turned out to be a betrayal of trust on a gargantuan scale.

Albert Grant

The son of an immigrant Jewish trader in Newgate Street, Albert Grant – born Abraham Gottheimer – was a true child of the City. But it was only after several false starts that he entered the business in which he was to make his (infamous) name.

That business was company promotion. Company promoters were people who formed companies and then sold shares in them to the public. Some promoters were reputable. Others were get-rich-quick fly-by-nights. The trouble with company promotion was that, of all business activities in the 19th century City, it offered the greatest possibilities for fraud. So extensively were these possibilities exploited that one historian has estimated that as many as one in six of all company promotions in the 19th century was fraudulent. A good many of them were the work of the notorious Albert Grant.

He entered the promotion business during the 1860s share boom, when it was easy to make money. He used all the usual tactics: paying fancy names to sit on his boards, promising unrealistically high dividends, and publishing misleading and sometimes deceptive information in his company prospectuses. But he also introduced some new methods of his own. He specialized in foreign companies – public works, mines, railways – which were difficult for investors to check out. And he deliberately targeted his promotions at small investors like widows and clergymen who were unversed in the ways of business and who were unlikely to challenge him if they felt they had been conned.

During his active company-promotion career, which lasted from 1863, when he was 33, until 1876, Grant promoted nearly forty companies and raised a total of about £25m. Much of this money was creamed off by Grant himself to fund his flamboyant lifestyle, which included bribing his way into Parliament and building the biggest private house in London (in Kensington, opposite the palace), with art collection to match. Substantial resources were also no doubt required to obtain the title of Baron, with which the King of Italy honoured him in 1868 and which caused much amusement in the City.

Probably Grant's most notorious promotion – and a classic example of his methodology – was the Emma Silver Mine Company, which was launched in 1871 with capital of £1m and predicted annual profits of £800,000. The mine, which was in Utah, USA, actually had little or no silver in it, and the company failed within a year. Investors lost virtually all their money – 99.75% to be precise. Grant walked away with £100,000.

The promotion that gave him the most trouble was another 1871 launch, the Lisbon Tramway Company, formed to develop what turned out to be an unworkable route between Lisbon and Sintra in Portugal. One aggrieved investor, named Twycross, was unwilling to take the company's failure lying down and sued Grant for publishing false information. Although the charge of fraud was not actually sustained at the trial, the mass resignation of Grant's legal team and the award of £700 in damages to Twycross were generally perceived to constitute a guilty verdict.

Grant's defeat in the case, which is still cited in English company law, destroyed public confidence in him and effectively ended his company-promotion career. When he tried to sell shares in a new banking company in 1878, only a quarter were taken up. He never moved into his palatial house (it was repossessed by the mortgage company and demolished in 1882, less than a decade after it had been started), and in 1879 he was declared bankrupt. Twenty years later he died but, for those who know Trollope's novel *The Way We Live Now* (1875), he lives on as the great swindler Augustus Melmotte.

Whitaker Wright

In the late 19th century a new breed of company promoters appeared on the scene – big players specializing in the launch of large-scale public companies.

Whitaker Wright was one of these. He spent the first half of his career in the US mining business, starting out by panning for gold in his own mine and rising to be chairman of the Philadelphia Mining Exchange. According to legend, he made and lost at least one fortune on the other side of the pond.

He arrived in London in 1889, aged 44, and set up in business as a mining company promoter in the middle of the Australian and South African mining booms. Like Robert Maxwell in more recent times, Wright was a physically big man who did everything on a similarly grand scale. His speciality was recruiting – or, should one say, bribing – big-name directors to sit on his boards. These sleeping partners were known as guinea-pigs because of both their ability to attract guineas from investors – their prime function – and their assumed greed. Wright's main vehicle, the London and Globe Finance Corporation, which was formed in 1897, had no fewer than four lords on its board, including – as chairman – the Marquis of Duffer in and Ava, a former governor-general of both Canada and India and ambassador to France.

The marquis and his colleagues did their work well, and the money rolled in. Within a few years Wright had his town house in Mayfair, his country house in Surrey (complete with glass-roofed billiard room under the lake) and his yacht at Cowes. The whole empire was controlled by the cigar-smoking, 16-stone Prince of Wales-lookalike from palatial offices at 43 Lothbury, next to the Bank of England.

Unlike the Bank of England, the Wright empire was not as solid as it seemed. In fact, by the late 1890s it was bankrupt. It stayed afloat only because the companies in the group bought and sold each other's shares to keep the prices up and because Wright borrowed wildly and falsified his companies' accounts.

But these desperate measures were not enough to counteract the slump in mining shares caused by the Boer War. Ten days after a shareholders' meeting at which the London and Globe announced a completely fictitious profit of £500,000, the company crashed with debts of over £700,000. The total deficiency of Wright's companies was over ten times that amount. Twenty stockbroking firms went to the wall with London and Globe, and thousands of investors were ruined.

Wright himself, however, thanks to limited liability, continued to live a life of luxury. But not for long. After a public outcry, he was extradited back to Britain from the USA – where he had fled under a false name in 1903 – and put on trial. He was convicted and sentenced at the Royal Courts of Justice in the Strand to seven years' penal servitude, but he, like Sadleir before him, could not face the disgrace. Stepping out to the lavatory, he returned to the private room allotted to him during his trial, drank a glass of whisky in the presence of his advisers – including Sir George Lewis, the royal solicitor – and collapsed, dead. He had swallowed a capsule of cyanide. Evidently he had been quite determined to put an end to himself because a loaded revolver was found in his pocket for use if the poison failed.

Every time you ride the Bakerloo line, think of this fallen giant: one of the more useful things he did was to put up the cash for its construction.

Horatio Bottomley

Like Whitaker Wright, the heroically named Horatio Bottomley was a massively successful mining-company promoter in the 1890s. But unlike Wright, when the mining market collapsed he survived, moving into different enterprises and continuing to make fortunes by shady means. It is therefore with truth that he has been called the most audacious (and last) of the great Victorian swindlers.

Bottomley first came to public notice in the 1880s when, having started out as a court reporter, he moved into promoting publishing companies. This phase of his career ended in bankruptcy in 1891 and allegations of fraud in 1893 but, not for the last time, he used his considerable oratorical gifts to talk his way out of trouble.

It was at this point that he moved into launching mining companies *à la* Grant and Wright, mainly in Australian gold. From his Joint Stock Institute in Broad Street Avenue in the City, Bottomley promoted nearly fifty companies with a total capital of £20m. They were all notoriously short-lived but, before they collapsed, Bottomley always made sure he got his cut. Fully £3m of that £20m is estimated to have gone into his own pocket. It was this money that bought him his racing stable – he was fond of a flutter – plus his luxurious apartment in Pall Mall (see the Mayfair and St James's walk, page 127), his country house in Sussex and his villa in the south of France, all prudently registered in his wife's name.

After mining, Bottomley moved into the closely linked worlds of journalism and politics by launching the *John Bull* newspaper and entering Parliament, both in 1906. Thanks to the disputes, scandals and legal actions which dogged his every footstep, his parliamentary career was somewhat chequered (revelations following his calculated voluntary bankruptcy in 1912 forced him to resign his seat). But *John Bull* (see the Covent Garden walk, page 88) did not let him down. It offered many possibilities for making a fast buck, and the almost unbelievably unscrupulous Bottomley exploited them to the full.

Before World War I, for example, he used the paper to promote a series of lotteries, based abroad because they were then illegal in Britain. Naturally Bottomley rigged the draws and pocketed the proceeds. After the war, when he had re-established his credibility and been re-elected to Parliament, he used the paper again to promote the Victory Bond Club. Ostensibly the club was formed to encourage purchase of the government's newly issued Victory War Bonds; in reality it was designed to enrich one H. Bottomley Esq., MP. Readers sent in their little bits of money, which he then pooled to buy bonds. Only he didn't use *all* the money to buy the bonds: some of it he withheld for himself – at least £150,000, and probably more, out of nearly £1m subscribed.

The scam was exposed by one of his enemies. In 1922 he was sentenced to a long-overdue term of penal servitude, which he served at Wormwood Scrubs prison in west London. Released after five years, he died a pauper in 1933, dependent on one of his many mistresses, his loyal wife having predeceased him in 1930. Bottomley deserves to be remembered most of all for the staggering hypocrisy with which he presented himself as the champion of the people while at the same time ripping those very same people off on a gigantic scale.

Clarence Hatry

Educated at St Paul's School, Clarence Hatry, the most notorious financier of the 1920s' City, would certainly not have regarded himself as a man of the people. Perhaps it was because of his middle-class origins that, though he used the vast wealth he so quickly amassed to buy all the usual trappings of success – the Mayfair town house (see the Mayfair and St James's walk, page 131), the country house, the yacht (said to be the second largest in the world) – he never seemed to value them very highly. Deal-making seems to have given him a greater thrill than wealth and, dare one say it, behind his asset-stripping and dawn-raiding there seems to have been some genuine commercial vision.

Hatry saw that what British industry needed most after World War I, if it was to compete successfully with the USA and other big economies, was rationalization. He therefore went into the rationalization business, buying up disparate companies and assembling them into groups, which he then sold off through share offerings to an unsuspecting public.

Like the mining and other companies promoted by his notorious predecessors, most of his groups were hugely and unsustainably overcapitalized, but he would make his own killing before they ultimately collapsed or had their capital drastically written down. What he was doing was, essentially, blowing up a bubble and keeping it inflated with constant draughts of fresh cash. When the flow of cash dried up, the bubble deflated and he went bust.

This happened in 1923, when his Commercial Corporation of London, based at 37–41 Gracechurch Street in the City, failed with liabilities of £3m. To his credit, Hatry attempted to pay off this huge sum by pumping in his own money and selling possessions. Perhaps this was why, a couple of years later, his creditors were prepared to advance him another wodge of cash so that he could re-enter the promotion business in a bid to pay off his outstanding debts. This must have seemed a risky strategy at the time. It certainly proved to be one.

After some initial success, Hatry, now operating through the Austin Friars Trust based at Pinners Hall in Old Broad Street, attempted the most ambitious deal of his career, the purchase of two big steel companies to form an even bigger one, which he intended to float as Steel Industries of Great Britain. Having raised £7.1m to buy the companies, Hatry needed just £0.9m more to complete the deal. But, try as he might, he just could not find those last few hundred thousand pounds. Desperate, he resorted to fraud.

He employed the same block of shares as collateral for loans from different branches of Lloyds Bank. He used companies which existed on paper only as collateral for further loans. And, worst of all, he forged municipal bonds. All might have been well had the stock market remained bullish. But a dramatic fall in autumn 1929 left him high and dry, his scams exposed for all to see. Investors lost £14m in his crash in September. The shock of his failure contributed to the Wall Street Crash on 25 October, which in turn sparked off the Great Depression. In January 1930 Hatry was sentenced to 14 years in prison for frauds which the trial judge said were 'the most appalling that have ever disfigured the commercial reputation of this country'. He was released after nine years. After World War II he built another business career, at one time owning the famous Hatchard's bookshop in Piccadilly.

THE CITY WALK

Start and finish:	Monument underground station (Circle and District lines).
Length:	2½ miles (4km).
Refreshments:	Various pubs, sandwich bars and take-aways all along the route. The ultra-modern glass–walled Zero Café at the foot of the old NatWest Tower (mentioned in the text) is conveniently sited at approximately the halfway point.
Route note:	The City is empty at weekends, so this walk is best done Monday to Friday.

Take the main (Fish Street Hill/Monument) exit from Monument station (⏷ left) and turn right to the **Monument**; this commemorates the notorious Great Fire of London, which destroyed huge swathes of the medieval city. Turn left into Monument Street and then right into Pudding Lane. The royal baker's shop where the Great Fire started in September 1666 was located somewhere in this lane, traditionally as far from the monument as the great stone pillar is high; i.e., 202ft (61.5m).

At the bottom of Pudding Lane cross Lower Thames Street, using the lights to the right, and turn left. Ahead on the right the Victorian building with the statue of Britannia high up above the entrance is the old

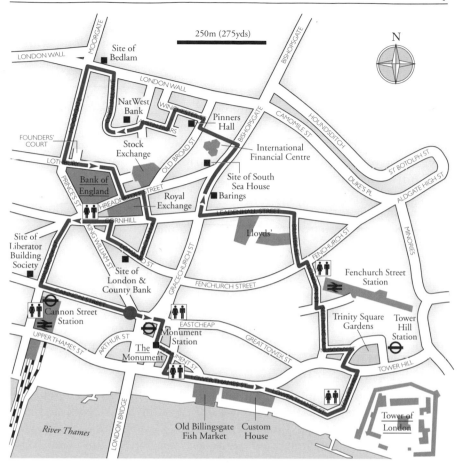

250m (275yds)

N

Billingsgate Fish Market, used until 1982, when it transferred to Docklands. The market's porters were so given to cursing and swearing that 'Billingsgate' became a synonym for bad language.

Beyond Billingsgate walk along past the frontage of the Custom House, keeping straight on when the road bends left up the hill. Cross Water Lane (view right to HMS *Belfast*) and continue past Sugar Quay. Eventually you come to the **Tower of London**. With thousands of tourists milling about, it's hard to believe that for centuries the Tower was a notorious prison and place of execution for traitors and other state prisoners (see page 28). Many of its inmates were brought by water, entering the castle via the riverside Traitors' Gate. The most notorious part of the prison today is the Bloody Tower, so called because it is believed that the Tower's most famous crime – the murder of the 12-year-old Edward V and his younger brother Prince

Richard, allegedly on the orders of their uncle, Richard III – was committed here in 1483. The Tower has witnessed several other notorious crimes, notably the poisoning of inconvenient courtier Sir Thomas Overbury by the wicked Countess of Essex in 1613 and the audacious theft of the Crown Jewels by Irish adventurer Colonel Blood in 1671 (see page 143).

In the 16th century, when religiously motivated spying and plotting were rife, torture was added to the list of Tower horrors. One Jesuit priest described the torture dungeon in the White Tower (the huge Norman keep in the centre of the castle) as a 'vast, shadowy place' with 'every device and instrument of human torture'. Apart from Little Ease, the cell where you could neither stand nor lie at full length, and the usual branding irons and thumbscrews, the main instruments were the rack and Skeffington's Daughter. The rack, introduced from the Continent in 1420, stretched you out until your joints parted. Skeffington's Daughter, on the other hand – invented by Sir Leonard Skeffington, lieutenant of the Tower in 1534 – clamped you together concertina-like until the blood burst out of your mouth, nose and the tips of your fingers.

Turn left up the hill (▥ left), with the Tower on your right. At the lights cross Tower Hill and continue on into Trinity Square. Just inside the gate on the right that leads into Trinity Square Gardens is the marked site of the Tower Hill scaffold, where more than 125 people were executed between the 14th and 18th centuries. The names of the most honourable are inscribed on plaques, starting with the Archbishop of Canterbury in 1381 and finishing with the Jacobite Lord Lovat in 1747. Not listed here is the notorious Mervyn Tuchet, 2nd Earl of Castlehaven, beheaded on 14 May 1631 for arranging and assisting at the rape of his wife by his servant, Brodway. This was just the last and arguably the worst of his crimes. He had also forced his wife to have sex with other servants, whom he also sodomized (buggery was a capital offence at this time). And he arranged for his stepdaughter to have sex with one of the same servants who had already had sex with the girl's mother – and this after arranging for the marriage of the girl, who was only 12, to his own son! Brodway and another household page, Lawrence Fitzpatrick, were also executed for the rape, but being commoners they were hanged at Tyburn.

Turn first left out of Trinity Square Gardens into Muscovy Street and follow it round to the right into Seething Lane. Pepys Garden, on the right, covers the site of the 17th century Navy Office where civil servant and notorious womanizer Samuel Pepys lived in the 1660s in an official Navy Office residence. From his famous diary it is clear that few women in London were safe from his lecherous attentions, even in church. Some he merely ogled; others he groped; a few he actually managed to bed.

These were mostly women whose husbands were dependent on him for promotion in the navy, financial men such as William Bagwell, who, thanks to his wife's affair with Pepys, rose from ordinary carpenter on a fifth-rate man o' war to master carpenter on a first-rate vessel. Here in Seething Lane Pepys frequently interfered with the maids of the house when they were going about their duties. His wife eventually found out about his infidelities on 25 October 1668 when she caught him with his hand up the skirt of her personal maid, Deb Willett.

At the end of Seething Lane turn left into Hart Street and then immediately right into New London Street. Go up the steps at the end and carry straight on into London Street (▥ on right). At the end of London Street cross Fenchurch Street at the lights and continue on into Billiter Street.

At Fenchurch Avenue look left to the new high-tech building of Lloyd's of London, the world-famous insurance market. When Lloyd's was in its previous building – the one with the large windows on the corner of Fenchurch Avenue – it was rocked by its worst-ever scandal, the PCW fraud. Over a ten-year period insurance underwriter Peter Cameron-Webb (PCW) and colleague Peter Dixon stole at least £38m from the syndicates of investors they represented in the insurance market. At the same time they also lost another £200m of their clients' money through a series of incompetent underwriting deals. When the scam (a complicated business involving re-insurance premiums) was exposed in 1983, the pair fled abroad, leaving their 3000 investors with what appeared to be a ruinous bill. In the end the industry stepped in to cover all but £34m of it. The PCW affair was just the first in a series of disasters for Lloyd's, the reverberations of which are still being felt today.

Carry on past the old Lloyd's and walk to the end of Billiter Street. On the other side of Leadenhall Street, No 100 was the head UK office of the Bank of Credit and Commerce International (BCCI) when that notoriously corrupt and ill-managed bank was summarily shut down by the Bank of England at 1.00pm on Friday 5 July 1991. It subsequently emerged that, as a result of the biggest fraud in world history, the BCCI, which claimed to have assets of $20 billion, in fact had debts of $4 billion. Some of that money belonged to the world's leading gangsters, drug-dealers and terrorists, whom BCCI had not scrupled to accept as customers. But most represented the savings of Asian businessmen, for whom the bank had been specifically set up in 1972. They had been systematically betrayed for at least seven years, the period for which the bank had been technically bankrupt before the fraud was exposed. The major architect of their betrayal was Abbas Gokal, head of the Gulf Shipping Group, which had illegally swallowed $1.2 billion of BCCI's money. In 1997 he was tried in Britain, fined £3m and jailed for 14 years. At the time of writing, liquidators are still involved in winding down the bank.

Turn left now on Leadenhall Street and walk to the junction with Bishopsgate. Here turn right. A little way along, by the bus stop, you come to No 8 Bishopsgate, until recently the historic address of one of Britain's most illustrious merchant banks, Barings. Rogue trader Nick Leeson made the name of Barings notorious in the mid-1990s when, as a trader on the Singapore Money Exchange, he brought the bank to its knees on 27 February 1995. Leeson, whose clever forgeries over a four-year period had enabled him to obtain and lose no less than £869m, was jailed in Singapore for six years but in July 1999 was released early for good behaviour. Meanwhile Dutch bank ING bought Barings for just £1 – though also having to shell out £650m to cover its debts.

Continue on along Bishopsgate as far as the junction with Threadneedle Street and look across to No 38 Threadneedle Street, on the far side. Now occupied by the Bank of Scotland, this building stands on the site of South Sea House, the office of the South Sea Company at the time of the South Sea Bubble, the most notorious financial scandal in British history. In 1720, in a bid to beat the Bank of England in a competition to take over the national debt, the company resorted to bribery, illegal share-support operations and other dubious practices on a massive scale in order to get the necessary legislation through Parliament. After the relevant Act was passed, South Sea stock rose to giddy heights, making fortunes for lucky speculators and sparking off a mania for company formations, many of which were downright swindles. One man set up a company 'to carry on an undertaking of great advantage, but nobody to know what it is'. He sold 1000 two-guinea shares in the morning and disappeared in the afternoon. Five months after the South Sea Act the bubble burst, shares crashed and thousands were ruined. Several South Sea Company directors and officials absconded abroad with their ill-gotten gains, but they were forced to pay a good deal of the money back, as were the Chancellor of the Exchequer and two other senior government ministers who were found to have accepted bribes. So traumatic was the Bubble for the City and the country that for over a century company formation was severely restricted and industrial growth accordingly hampered. Perhaps it is not surprising that the City has not yet got round to putting a plaque on the building to commemorate this hugely significant historical event.

Now cross at the lights to 13 Bishopsgate (the round-ended building next to the Bank of Scotland) and turn right. Under the overhead walkway turn left and walk through the Bishopsgate complex of the National Westminster Bank and past the glass-walled Zero Café in the base of what used to be the NatWest Tower. On Old Broad Street turn right. Opposite, at 105–108 Old Broad Street, is modern Pinners Hall. In an earlier version of this building the 1920s financier Clarence Hatry ran the Austin Friars Trust, whose collapse – as we saw earlier this chapter (see page 47) – contributed to the 1929 Wall Street Crash.

Just beyond Pinners Hall turn left into Great Winchester Street. Near the far end turn left by the railings into Austin Friars Passage and then right into Austin Friars. On the right steps lead up to 15 Austin Friars. This is the actual building where Whitaker Wright ran his London and Globe Finance Corporation before moving to the office in Lothbury where he crashed in 1900. (The walk passes the site of the Lothbury office shortly.)

Continue past the steps, through the gate and out onto Throgmorton Avenue, opposite another NatWest bank building. This major British bank was embroiled in a scandal in the heady days of the 1980s when its then merchant-banking arm, County NatWest, based here at 12 Throgmorton Avenue, was involved in the notorious Blue Arrow affair, a takeover that went wrong and resulted in the second-longest criminal trial in English legal history. Using NatWest money, the relatively tiny Blue Arrow (City office: 16 Finsbury Circus) took over US recruitment giant Manpower in 1987. When Blue Arrow's subsequent share offer flopped, it couldn't pay NatWest back. In order to support the share price, Blue Arrow's merchant bank County NatWest stepped in and bought three times the amount of Blue Arrow's shares it was legally permitted to hold without declaring its stake, which of course it failed to do. This dubious operation came to light when stock markets around the world crashed on Black Monday, 19 October 1987. In the subsequent trial, three County NatWest bankers were convicted, but the verdicts were overturned by the Court of Appeal on the grounds that, because the trial had gone on for so long (a year), they could not be regarded as sound. So another £40m of public money went down the drain.

Turn left on Throgmorton Avenue and then first right into Copthall Avenue, and follow this round to the right and on to the end, where it meets London Wall. In the 18th century London's main lunatic asylum occupied a large site on the opposite side of this road. Going to see the idiots at Bedlam (a corruption of Bethlehem, from Bethlehem Royal Hospital) was one of the things you did if you came on a visit to the capital. Once you had paid your twopence, you 'were suffered, unattended, to run rioting up and down the wards, making sport and diversion of the miserable inhabitants'. The hospital finally stopped indulging what the poet William Cowper called the 'cruel curiosity of holiday ramblers' in 1770.

Turn left on London Wall and walk as far as the traffic lights (🚇 ahead to the right in Fore Street). Turn left into Moorgate. When you get to Moorgate Place on the left, the modern office block across the road stands on the site of No 49, which in the 1920s was the building occupied by Arcos, the All-Russian Co-operative Society. Arcos was supposed to promote trade between Britain and the new Soviet Union, but in reality it was one of the Soviets' main international spy bases and subversion centres. Police raided the building on 12 May 1927, discovering crates of rifles ('manufacturers' samples') in a steel-doored basement room, plus piles of incriminating documents. However, certain key papers were missing, leading to the suspicion that a never-identified mole in Scotland Yard had tipped the Soviets off in advance.

Carry on along Moorgate. A little further on you come to Copthall Close, on the left. Opposite here in the 19th century were the offices of the Great Northern Railway, at 14 Moorgate. In the 1850s the GNR was the victim of a sensational fraud when its own registrar, Leopold Redpath, forged fictitious stock worth £240,000s of and used the dividends to fund a lavish lifestyle, with a town house in Regent's Park and a country house in Surrey. The fraud only came to light when the chairman of the company was surprised to see a certain peer, to whom he was talking on a railway platform, raise his hat and exchange greetings when Redpath came along. Asked what he knew of Redpath, the peer replied only that he was a charming fellow who gave the best dinners in London. How, wondered the chairman, was this possible when Redpath's regular salary was just £300 a year? Redpath was duly convicted of embezzlement and transported for life.

At the end of Moorgate turn left into Lothbury. On the left you pass Founders' Court, where infamous company promoter Albert Grant tried to revive his banking business following his bankruptcy in 1879. Beyond the church, the building on the east corner of Tokenhouse Yard covers the site of 43 Lothbury, where Whitaker Wright's London and Globe Finance Corporation was based when it collapsed in 1900, leading ultimately to Wright's suicide. Now turn right into Bartholomew Lane. On the right are the **Bank of England** and the entrance to the bank's museum. On the left is Capel Court, historically the main entrance to the London Stock Exchange.

Both these institutions have been the victims of notorious frauds in their day. In 1814 the Stock Exchange was taken for a ride by an adventurer named Berenger, who engineered a sudden rise in stocks by convincing the City that the Allies had won the war against Napoleon. The hoax lasted for only a day, but that was long enough to make a killing. For various reasons (see page 133) it appeared at the time as though Lord Cochrane, MP, naval officer and son of an earl, was behind the fraud, and he was duly convicted and imprisoned. It was only years later after he had inherited his title and won fame as a naval commander in South American independence wars that he was able to return to England and clear his name.

In 1872 a gang of well known American forgers and impostors spotted a glaring weakness in the way the Bank of England handled bills of exchange (rather similar to travellers' cheques). Exploiting this weakness, they soon cleared £100,000. The fraud was discovered when they forgot to date a couple of bills, and all four culprits got penal servitude for life (though none served longer than 18 years).

In March 1995 scandal hit the Bank again when the male deputy governor was caught *in flagrante delicto* with a female financial journalist on the floor of the governor's dressing room. This being England, the deputy governor resigned immediately. The incident inspired one of the *The Sun* newpaper's most memorable headlines: 'The Bonk of England.'

Carry on along Bartholomew Lane. At the end turn left into Threadneedle Street and then right into Royal Exchange Buildings. At Cornhill turn left and cross at the lights into Birchin Lane. No 25 on the left, now a wine bar, was the offices of the Mercantile Discount Company from 1859 until its collapse two years later. This was one of several ventures Albert Grant – then still Albert Gottheimer – tried before finding his true vocation as a promoter of worthless companies. Just beyond Bengal Court, a plaque on the left where the street frontage recedes commemorates retired naval captain Ralph Binney, who was killed in 1944 while trying to prevent the getaway of a gang who had just robbed a jeweller's in Birchin Lane. Having stood in front of their car, he was run over and dragged underneath it for over a mile before being flung clear. He died in hospital soon after. Ronald Hedley, the car driver, was sentenced to death but reprieved. One of the gang was later hanged for killing a man in Charlotte Street in the West End (see page 118).

At the end of Birchin Lane you come to Lombard Street, London's historic banking quarter (the earliest City bankers came from Lombardy in northern Italy). On the corner where you are standing (right-hand side of Birchin Lane), Overend and Gurney had their offices in the mid-19th century. Known as The Banker's Banker and second only in importance to the Bank of England, the firm lost millions in bad loans in the 1850s and so floated as a public company in 1865 to raise more capital. But the directors neglected to tell investors about the earlier debts and the company crashed on Black Friday, 11 May 1866, ruining thousands and precipitating a financial crisis of gigantic proportions. Three years later six directors were acquitted of defrauding shareholders of £3m. The bank's debts were not finally discharged until 1893.

Opposite Overend and Gurney, on the south side of Lombard Street, Albert Grant and his brother Maurice ran Grant Brothers, the private bank that Albert used as the vehicle for his company promotions when he was at the height of his fame in the 1870s.

Turn right now into Lombard Street. On the left a new office block stands on the site of 21 Lombard Street, midway between Nicholas Lane and Abchurch Lane. This was the address of the London and County Bank, which the swindler and forger John Sadleir chaired until his exposure in 1856. Directly opposite, on the east corner of Change Alley, stood Glyn's Bank, at 67 Lombard Street. Glyn's was the London agent of Sadleir's family bank in Ireland, and here he used to pick up cash remitted to him from Ireland. It was when Glyn's refused to give him any more money that Sadleir, realizing the game was up, committed suicide on Hampstead Heath.

Beyond Abchurch Lane on the left is Post Office Court. Here in 1902 Kitty Byron drew a knife from her muff and stabbed her lover, stockbroker Arthur Baker, to death. She was found guilty of murder but, because of the circumstances of the case (Baker was a bully and a drunkard and beat her up regularly), she was reprieved and released from prison after six years.

Walk on past the Post Office and, just before the end of Lombard Street, turn right into Pope's Head Alley and then left on Cornhill. No 14 Cornhill, on your immediate left (then Nos 17 and 18), was where Albert Grant started out as a company promoter in 1864, operating through the predecessor of Grant Brothers, the Crédit Foncier et Mobilier. In his first three years he launched eleven major enterprises, netting himself a fortune of £500,000 and earning a reputation with the public (if not with more sceptical City men) as a wheeler-dealer with the Midas touch.

Carry on down to the end of Cornhill (🚇 in Bank station subway). On your left is a round-ended building that stands on the site of the home and business of 18th century printer and publisher Thomas Guy. Guy was one of those who made a fortune out of the South Sea Bubble: he used it to found the eponymous hospital that still operates in Southwark. Later the Globe Assurance Company was based here. An extraordinary fraud on this company came to light in 1850 when Walter Watts, the senior clerk in the cashier's office, was found to have embezzled more than £70,000 over six years in order to fund a second life as a playwright and theatrical impresario. He had even leased two theatres himself, something he certainly wouldn't have been able to do on his regular salary of £200 a year. In a tragic dénouement worthy of the opera of which he was so fond, Watts killed himself in prison, having been sentenced to 10 years' transportation.

Still standing on this corner, look over to the right to Prince's Street. No 2 Prince's Street, now buried beneath the large NatWest Bank

Plate 11: *The Tower of London: state prison, place of torture and execution, and scene of more than one notorious crime (see pages 28 and 49).*

Plate 12: The executioner's block, axe and mask in the Tower of London (see pages 28 and 50).

Plate 13: Rogue trader Nick Leeson is arrested in Frankfurt after breaking Barings bank (see page 52).

Plate 14: A typical thieves' kitchen and drinking den, once common in such notorious places as Ram Alley, off Fleet Street, and rookeries like Saffron Hill and St Giles (see pages 33, 36 and 87).

Plate 15: *Bedlam, London's main lunatic asylum, was a popular attraction for tourists in the 18th century (see page 53).*

Plate 16: *A scene from the 1936 Battle of Cable Street when fascists' attempts to march through the East End led to widespread rioting (see page 72).*

POLICE · BUDGET · EDITION   EDITED · BY · HAROLD FURNISS

FAMOUS CRIMES

PAST · AND · PRESENT   ONE · PENNY

THE DISCOVERY OF "JACK THE RIPPER'S" FIRST MURDER.

Vol. II. – No. 15.

Plate 17: *Labourer John Reeves finds the body of 39-year-old prostitute Martha Tabram on the first-floor landing of 37 George Yard Buildings. Martha is believed to have been Jack the Ripper's first victim (see pages 60 and 66).*

building on the corner, was the address of the Union Bank of London in 1860 when it was revealed that William Pullinger, its chief cashier, had over a five-year period defrauded his employers of £263,000, fully half what the bank thought it had on reserve at the Bank of England across the road. All the money went on wild speculations on the Stock Exchange. Pullinger went to prison for 20 years but the bank survived to become – like John Sadleir's London and County Bank – part of today's NatWest Bank.

From this corner at the beginning of Cornhill, turn left, cross Lombard Street and turn right in front of the Mansion House (the Lord Mayor of London's official residence). At the far end of the building look ahead right to the huge HSBC Bank building on the north side of Poultry. The pillared entrance in the centre marks the site of a court which once led to the Poultry Compter, one of the two prisons in the City belonging to the City's sheriffs. The Poultry was no better than any of the other prisons described in more detail in Chapter Two. In 1776, four years after it had housed the last black slave to be imprisoned in England, it was described by its unofficial prison doctor as 'very dirty, old, confined and extremely unhealthy. Men and women, felons and disorderly people, are crammed together in one ward in the day, and at night lie on dirty boards in filthy holes almost unfit for swine. In this prison riot, drunkenness, blasphemy and debauchery echo from the walls; sickness and misery are confined within them.' The Poultry Compter, founded in medieval times, was closed in 1815 and replaced by a new prison on a different site.

Turn left round the corner of the Mansion House and walk down Walbrook to the end, where it meets Cannon Street. On the right, a massive new corner office block (Bucklersbury House) stands on the site of several former buildings, including 20 Budge Row (roughly opposite the Aroma Coffee House at 70 Cannon Street), where Jabez Balfour had his Liberator Building Society and London and General Bank in the 1870s and 1880s. Turn left into Cannon Street (⛎ in station on right) and walk for some way until you come to a junction of five roads. Here go straight on across King William Street and then round the corner in front of the Standard Chartered Bank at 37–41 Gracechurch Street. This is the last notorious site on the walk: Clarence Hatry's Commercial Corporation of London was based here when it went bust in 1923, so bringing to an ignominious end the first phase of the career of the fraudster whose much bigger crash in 1929 contributed to the onset of the Great Depression.

Using the lights in front of the Standard Chartered, cross to the central traffic island (⛎) and then turn right and cross Eastcheap into Fish Street Hill. Monument station, where the walk ends, is on the right.

The East End
Murder and Mayhem

Immediately east of the City of London lies the capital's historic working-class and manufacturing district, known as the East End. It neatly balances the upper-class residential – but now largely business – district at the other end of central London, the West End.

In the 19th century extreme poverty and appalling living conditions made the area notorious as a hotbed of crime and vice. Waves of immigration – particularly by Jews following European pogroms – did not help. Things have improved this century, but slum clearances, highway improvements and post-Blitz rebuilding have seriously weakened the famous community spirit that once sustained the East End through many hard times.

The notorious history of the East End is dominated by just two names: Jack the Ripper and the Krays. Jack the Ripper was a serial killer active in the Whitechapel district on the edge of the City in the late 1880s. The Krays, hailing from Bethnal Green, just beyond Whitechapel, were London's principal gangland bosses north of the Thames in the 1960s.

Jack the Ripper
For a number of years after Queen Victoria's Golden Jubilee in 1887, Whitechapel was terrorized by a series of brutal attacks on women, many of which were fatal. The fatalities are generally known as the Whitechapel Murders. No one knows who carried out either the attacks or the murders, but a number of the murders – almost certainly five, possibly six and perhaps eight – have been ascribed to one anonymous individual, the notorious Jack the Ripper.

Over the past forty years or so the Jack the Ripper industry has produced a deluge of books, articles and TV programmes. Most can be discounted as rubbish, especially those making the more preposterous suggestions – such as that the murders were committed by the queen's doctor inside a special death carriage in an attempt to cover up a scandal involving one of her sons. But mixed up in all the garbage is some fine historical research, and also some thoughtful insights.

These insights, together with his own painstaking research work, have enabled the latest and best writer on the subject, Philip Sugden, to profile the man he believes the police should have been looking for in the teeming streets of Whitechapel more than a century ago. According to Sugden, the murderer was probably a local man, white but possibly of continental origin, in his 20s or 30s. He was dressed respectably and of average or less than average height. He was single, in regular employment, right-handed and possessed some degree of anatomical knowledge and surgical skill.

The Ripper operated by making contact with prostitutes in the street and then going with them to some dark corner, such as an unlit back yard or the corner of a square, for sex, which in assignations of this kind was usually performed in the open air and standing up. But, before sex started, he noiselessly strangled his victims, lowered them to the ground and cut their throats right down to the spinal cord. Then he carried out the mutilations which earned him his unenviable sobriquet. In three cases he also took body parts away when he left the scene of the crime.

After such butchery it would seem reasonable to assume that he must have been drenched in gore. However, the modern consensus is that, because of the way he worked — cutting throats from left to right, for example — he was unlikely to have been seriously bloodstained. This must be correct — or, at least, it is tempting to say it must be — because otherwise it is difficult to see how he could have made his getaway without someone noticing or without, say, leaving bloody footprints. One of the many extraordinary things about the Ripper is the way he was able to commit his crimes unheard and unseen and then to disappear, apparently into thin air, without leaving any trace of his presence apart from the body of his victim.

Jack the Ripper got his sobriquet from the signature on two notes sent to a news agency at the height of the scare. It is possible that the notes were sent by the killer, but the 'Jack the Ripper' name bears all the hallmarks of a press label, and the general view is that the notes were in fact hoaxes perpetrated by a freelance journalist named Best who was covering the Ripper story for the *Star* newspaper. Whoever invented the name, it has stuck and, even if the so-far-anonymous Whitechapel murderer of 1888 is one day identified, he will probably never be able to shake off the name by which he now universally known.

Serious 'ripperologists' refer to the core murders more or less definitely ascribed to the Ripper as the 'canonical five'. However, Metropolitan Police Inspector Frederick Abberline, who was in charge of detectives on the ground during the murder investigation, believed that the killing of Martha Tabram, which preceded the canonical five by some three weeks, was also the Ripper's work. She is therefore included in the following list of the Ripper's victims, giving him — for the purposes of this book — a total of six.

Martha Tabram

A 39-year-old prostitute estranged from her husband, Martha had lived with William Turner for ten years, off and on – more off than on because of her drinking. At the time of her death the relationship was in an off phase. Martha was last seen just before midnight on Bank Holiday Monday, 6 August 1888, when she went into George Yard for sex with a soldier she had picked up in a local pub. Her body was found on the first-floor landing of the George Yard Buildings tenement at 4.50 the next morning by labourer John Reeves as he set off for work. Medical examination showed that she had died about 2.30am as the result of a frenzied knife attack, during which she had been stabbed 39 times (but not mutilated). One of the stab wounds appeared to have been inflicted using a bayonet-type weapon, raising the possibility that there was a connection between her soldier client and her death.

Mary Ann Nichols

Forty-two-year-old Mary Ann Nichols – Polly to her friends – was married with five children, but had been separated from her family since 1880, the year after the birth of her last child. Like most of her fellow victims, she earned money through prostitution and spent it on drink and a bed at the doss-house. On the night of her death she had already earned and spent her doss money three times and, when last seen – drunk and staggering – by a friend at 2.30am on 31 August 1888, she was going out to earn it for a fourth time. An hour and ten minutes later her body was found outside a school in Buck's Row by Police Constable John Neill. Her throat had been cut twice, the second cut almost severing her head from her body. She was the first victim to be mutilated and is therefore regarded by Ripper students as the killer's first definite victim. Her skirts had been pushed up and her abdomen ripped open to expose her intestines. She was buried in Ilford cemetery on 6 September.

Annie Chapman

Forty-seven-year-old Annie Chapman abandoned her husband and three children in Windsor in the early 1880s and came to London, where she earned a precarious living selling – besides her body – matches, flowers and her own crochet work. She was last seen outside 29 Hanbury Street haggling with a respectably – but shabbily – dressed man at 5.30am on Saturday 8 September 1888. Half an hour later one of the many occupants of the house, Leadenhall market porter John Davis, found her body in the backyard. Her throat had been cut, her dress pushed up and her intestines ripped out and strewn across her left shoulder. A post mortem subsequently showed that her uterus was missing. She was buried secretly by her family at Manor Park on 14 September.

Among several items found near her body was a leather apron. This chimed in with a current scare in the district about a man who was going around threatening and blackmailing prostitutes; he wore a leather apron and was actually nicknamed Leather Apron. The man was successfully identified, but was ruled out as a Ripper suspect after the murder-scene apron was found to belong to a likewise innocent resident of 29 Hanbury Street.

Elizabeth Stride

Born in Sweden in 1843, Elizabeth Gustafsdotter came to England in 1866 and married a carpenter named John Stride. After the marriage broke down in 1882, Elizabeth descended into the doss-house world of prostitution and drunkenness (for which she was convicted eight times in 1887–8). Soon after midnight on Saturday 29 September 1888 she was seen several times in Berner Street with various men. At 1.00am on Sunday morning her body was found at the entrance to Dutfield's Yard, behind 40 Berner Street, by Louis Diemschütz, steward of the adjacent International Working Men's Educational Club. Her throat had been cut, but that was her only injury. However, it is thought that the murderer had intended to mutilate her as usual but was scared off by the arrival of Diemschütz in his pony and trap. Elizabeth was buried in a pauper's grave in the East London cemetery.

Catherine Eddowes

Baulked in Berner Street, it is presumed the Ripper stepped out smartly in a westerly direction to Mitre Square, in the City, in search of another victim, for the dreadfully mutilated body of Catherine Eddowes was found there less than an hour later.

Having spent the evening sobering up in a cell in Bishopsgate police station, Catherine – separated from her partner and three children for the last eight years – was last seen at 1.35am at one of the entrances to Mitre Square, talking amicably to a man and with her hand on his chest. Just ten minutes later Police Constable Watkins of the City Police found her body at the southwest corner of the square. This time, in addition to the usual injuries, her face had been severely mutilated. Moreover, her uterus and left kidney were later found to be missing. Catherine was buried in an unmarked grave in Ilford cemetery on 8 October.

Mary Jane Kelly

Born in Ireland, 25-year-old Mary Kelly grew up in Wales and married a miner. After his death in a pit accident, she came to London and worked in a West End brothel before moving to the East End. She was last seen alive at 2.00am on Friday 9 November 1888, picking up a client in Commercial Street and taking him back to her ground-floor room in Miller's Court behind 26 Dorset Street, Spitalfields. She was probably killed about 4.00am, but her naked body was not found until 10.45am, when the rent collector called. With time and privacy, the killer had been able to mutilate her much more severely than any previous victim. Bits of her were found on the bedside table and under the bed. Her breasts had been cut off and her face was cut up beyond recognition. It was subsequently discovered that her heart was missing. Mary was buried in Walthamstow Roman Catholic cemetery on 19 November 1888.

Mary Kelly was the Ripper's last definite victim. Some people think that after the Miller's Court orgy he either died, was committed to an asylum as a madman or possibly committed suicide. However, in the three following years there were two more murders which bore some Ripper hallmarks. After 1891 there were no more Ripper-style murders in Whitechapel and in 1892 – the year in which Inspector Abberline retired – the Metropolitan Police finally closed their file on the case. It has been reopened many times since, but to little effect.

The Krays

Half a century after Jack the Ripper stalked the streets of Whitechapel, Violet Kray gave birth to boy twins at 64 Stene Street, Hoxton, a couple of miles north of Ripper territory. One was called Reggie and the other Ronnie. Violet already had another son, Charlie, born seven years earlier. Violet was married, but since her husband was away most of the time she was virtually a single mother, so in 1939, just before war broke out, she moved southeast to Vallance Road, off Whitechapel Road, where her family, the Lees, was based. Here, with lots of help from her family and occasional assistance from her husband when he wasn't dodging the police as a wartime deserter, she brought her children up.

Despite doting on their big-hearted mother, the Kray twins were hard men from the start. As young teenagers they were notorious neighbourhood gang leaders and streetfighters and also unusually successful boxers. In fact, both could probably have made it as professionals in the ring had not National Service intervened. They hated being in the army, and most of their two-year stretch in the ranks was spent either on the run or in some kind of military confinement.

After nine months in an army prison the 20-year-old twins returned to the East End in 1954 determined on a life of crime. In effect they had been criminals since the age of 12 when they had had their first brush with the law. But it wasn't until they were faced with the prospect of having to earn a living that they decided crime was a far easier route to the fame and fortune they both craved than either a regular job or training every day and fighting in the ring at night.

In true gangster fashion, they began by taking over a run-down snooker hall in Eric Street, Mile End. They built this up as a source of income and also used it as a base for their growing gang, which became known as the Firm, and their various criminal operations. In time these came to include protection rackets, drinking clubs, gambling clubs, drugs, pornography, fruit machines and what were called long-firm frauds – business swindles whereby apparently legitimate businesses established credentials with a wholesaler, bought a large amount of stock on credit, sold it off cheap for cash and then disappeared overnight. With Ronnie's genius for planning – a talent which earned him his nickname, The Colonel – and Reggie's aptitude for business, these underworld activities soon became extremely lucrative.

The twins consciously modelled themselves on their hero Billy Hill (see page 110), one of the two dominant figures in London's post-war gangland. But what really set them apart from the competition, of which there was plenty, was their willingness to use casual violence to expand their criminal empire. By all accounts they could scare the living daylights out of people just by being themselves. But, if intimidation and threats failed to do the trick, then they were quite prepared to resort to force. As boxers they were used to it. Ronnie, homosexual, complex and mentally unstable, was the more violent of the two. He spent hours sharpening his many knives and swords on a grindstone set up in the yard at Vallance Road, and he seems to have positively enjoyed inflicting pain on others, using either fists or blades. As events were to show, he was also desperate to try a gun. The twins had had at least one pistol stashed under the floorboards at Vallance Road since they were 16.

In 1957 the twins suffered a setback when Ronnie went to prison for beating up a rival gang member in a Stepney pub. However, his absence allowed Reggie to come out from the shadow of his dominant brother and begin building up the Firm's club empire, starting with the Double R drinking club in Bow Road. It is said that in time the twins came to own or have a stake in thirty clubs and bars. Many of them had been mysteriously firebombed just before the Krays took over!

After a serious breakdown in gaol, during which he was diagnosed schizophrenic and certified insane, Ronnie was if anything more violent when he came out. While Reggie now favoured more subtle methods of developing their business interests, Ronnie urged even greater use of threats and violence as tools of expansion. Around 1960 his policy produced spectacular results when the twins 'frightened' the owner of a smart Knightsbridge gambling club in Wilton Place into letting them buy the establishment. For an outlay of just £1000 the twins got a business turning over £500,000 a year and personal incomes of £40,000 a year, huge sums for the time. All they had to do for the money was turn up from time to time in a black tie. As a host to greet the punters they employed down-at-heel peer Lord Effingham, who was only too willing to sell his name for a regular income.

With their takeover of Esmeralda's Barn and their subsequent move from this launchpad into protection and other rackets in the West End, the Krays became undoubted kings of London's gangland. As Reggie himself said, Carnaby Street ruled fashion, the Beatles and the Rolling Stones ruled pop, and the Krays ruled London. They rubbed shoulders with celebrities, MPs, peers and other members of the Establishment, and in the East End they were fêted as heroes and benefactors. Yet at the same time they were the most feared gangsters in the country.

The Krays' move into the West End brought them into conflict with the Richardsons, their main rivals for control of London's criminal underworld. The Richardson gang, as dominant in South London as the Krays were in the East End, was run by scrap-metal dealers Eddie and Charlie Richardson, with George Cornell and Mad Frankie Fraser acting as first lieutenants. In March 1966 a gun battle involving the Richardsons at a South London club resulted in the death of Dickie Hart, cousin and ally of the Krays. No one knows who actually shot Hart, but many believe it was Cornell.

Soon after the battle, word was brought to Ronnie Kray by one of his many spies that Cornell was drinking in the nearby Blind Beggar pub, a rash thing to do as it was right in the middle of the Krays' manor. Cornell was already a marked man for calling Ronnie a 'fat poof'; Ronnie may also have believed the rumours that Cornell killed his cousin. Picking up a gun, Ronnie went straight to the Blind Beggar, walked up to Cornell at the bar and shot him in the head. Several people saw him do it, but when questioned by the police they remembered nothing. Such was the control the Krays exercised through their reign of terror in the East End.

Later in 1966 the twins, who could be extraordinarily generous to their own kind, sprung gentle giant Frank Mitchell, alias the Mad Axeman, from Dartmoor prison. Having been secreted in a Barking flat and told to keep his head down, Mitchell grew restless and started to cause trouble. The Krays ordered him to be taken care of. On Christmas Eve 1966 Fred Foreman shot him in the back of a van. Apparently it took 12 bullets to finish him off.

Foreman was subsequently acquitted of the murder at the Old Bailey, but he has since admitted that he did indeed shoot Mitchell – as a favour to the Krays.

After the Cornell killing, Ronnie Kray boasted about it endlessly and is said to have goaded his brother into carrying out a murder of his own. Whether as a result of the goading or not – and Reggie himself denied it – the fact is that a year and a half later Reggie Kray too became a killer when he murdered Jack 'the Hat' McVitie in a basement flat in Evering Road, Stoke Newington.

A small-time crook who had taken money from the Krays, joked about them and even apparently threatened to shoot them, McVitie – called 'the Hat' because he was sensitive about his bald patch and always wore a hat to conceal it – was in Ronnie's sights by October 1967. What seems to have happened is that Reggie decided he must take care of McVitie himself, perhaps for the sake of his own honour in the Firm. McVitie was accordingly lured to the Stoke Newington flat and attacked. Reggie first tried to shoot him but the gun jammed. Grabbing a knife he stabbed him instead, the final thrust transfixing McVitie's throat and pinning him to the floor. The police later recovered the knife and jammed gun from the canal near Queensbridge Road, but McVitie's body was never found. In fact, none of the bodies of the Krays' three known victims was ever discovered.

While the twins celebrated McVitie's death with a short holiday in Cambridge and East Anglia, the police decided that the time had come to take action against the Krays. Over the winter months and into the spring of 1968 the formidable Inspector 'Nipper' Read of Scotland Yard put together a case against them. The hope was that, once the twins were in custody, the wall of silence that had so far protected them would collapse. In a series of dawn raids on 8 May 1968 the Kray gang was rounded up by the police. The twins were found at their mother's council flat in Braithwaite House, Old Street. Reggie was in bed with a girl, and Ronnie with a boy.

In January 1969 the Kray case finally came to court. The police strategy had worked, and several key witnesses, including the barmaid of the Blind Beggar, came forward. Ronnie Hart, cousin of the Krays, turned Queen's Evidence to testify about the McVitie murder. On 8 March 1969 the twins were found guilty and sentenced to at least 30 years in prison. Seven other members of the Firm, including the twins' elder brother Charlie, were also convicted. Only one was acquitted.

Ronnie Kray served almost 28 years before dying of a heart attack in Broadmoor on 17 March 1995, aged 61. Charlie Kray died in April 2000 having been convicted of drug dealing in 1997 at the age of 70 and sent to prison again. Reggie Kray served more than 30 years before being released a few weeks before his death in September 2000.

The Krays were the last in the series of gangs that dominated London's underworld over the half-century from the 1920s to the 1960s. Fortunately they have had no successors, and it is now doubtful – despite the power of organized crime – whether they ever will have.

THE EAST END WALK

Start and finish: Aldgate East underground station (District and Hammersmith & City lines).

Length: 3¾ miles (6km).

Refreshments: The Blind Beggar pub, where Ronnie Kray shot George Cornell, serves lunchtime food and is at the halfway stage, and so is an obvious place to stop, but it is nothing special in itself and its interior is completely different from what it was at the time of the killing. Near the beginning of the walk, Brick Lane is famous for its Asian restaurants, and towards the end the Houndsditch area has many sandwich bars and take-aways catering to City office workers.

Take the 'High Street (north side)' exit from Aldgate East underground station and turn left. Cross Commercial Street at the lights and continue along Whitechapel High Street. After a while you come to the White Hart pub, on the left. In 1890 Severin Klosowski, a qualified junior surgeon from Poland who came to England in 1887 and worked as a hairdresser in the East End, kept a barber shop in the basement of this pub. Later, in 1903, having changed his name to George Chapman and turned to pub-keeping in Southwark, he was hanged for poisoning three women (see page 18). After Chapman's arrest, Inspector Abberline, head of the Whitechapel Murders investigation, thought it possible he might have been the Jack the Ripper, but his preferred method of killing suggests otherwise and there is no actual evidence to link him with the Ripper's crimes.

Just beyond the pub, turn left through the archway into Gunthorpe Street (note the tiled history display on the left of the arch and, further on, the painted board on the side of the pub mentioning Klosowski-alias-Chapman). In the Ripper's day this street was called George Yard. Still narrow and cobbled, it retains more of its original appearance and atmosphere than any other Ripper-associated site. Near the far end, on the left, the red-brick Sunley House stands on the site of George Yard Buildings, the tenement block where Martha Tabram, possibly the Ripper's first victim, was murdered in the early hours of 7 August 1888.

When you get to Wentworth Street, turn left and then cross right to go through the gate into Flower and Dean Walk. Flower and Dean Walk takes its name from Flower and Dean Street, one of several streets which in the 1880s formed a notorious rookery or criminal quarter. This was the milieu in which the Ripper's victims lived and in which he operated. The local clergyman described it as the 'wicked quarter mile' because of its many prostitutes. Most of these prostitutes – including the Ripper's victims – lodged in the rookery's numerous doss-houses, where beds could be hired for a few pence a night.

When you reach the crossroads in the middle of this modern housing development, turn left and carry on along Thrawl Street, another of the rookery's more notorious streets. At the end turn right into Commercial Street. The first street you come to on the right is Lolesworth Close: this is the only remaining part of the original Flower and Dean Street. At least three of the Ripper's victims lodged here at one time or another. The eastern part of the old street is now covered by the Attlee Adventure Playground.

Carry on along Commercial Street, crossing the entrance to Fashion Street. When you get to the disused drinking fountain set into the churchyard railings on the right, look left along the 'Private Road' between White's Row car park on the left and the old Fruit and Wool Exchange (once part of Spitalfields Market) on the right. In the Ripper's time this road, towards the northern end of the 'wicked quarter mile', was called Dorset Street. Miller's Court, where Mary Kelly – supposed to be the Ripper's final victim – was murdered, was about one-third of the way along the street on the right-hand (north) side. Dorset Street was renamed Duval Street before, in 1929, being demolished to make way for an extension to Spitalfields Market.

Carry on past the churchyard to Fournier Street. The Ten Bells pub on the corner, here in Ripper times, was a favourite drinking haunt of Annie Chapman, Elizabeth Stride, Catherine Eddowes and Mary Kelly. Turn right into Fournier Street and first left into Wilkes Street. At the end of Wilkes Street, turn right into Hanbury Street. A disused brewery completely fills the north side of this street but many original houses remain on the south side. No 29 Hanbury Street – the house where Annie Chapman, believed to be the Ripper's third victim, was killed on 8 September 1888 – was on the north side roughly opposite the present-day Nos 28 and 30.

Carry on to Brick Lane. Turn left and walk along to the railway bridge. Just beyond it, take the second right into Cheshire Street. Cheshire Street eventually turns into Dunbridge Street. A short distance after that, Dunbridge Street joins Vallance Road at a roundabout by the railway line. The modern version of the original 178 Vallance Road, where the Kray twins lived with their mother while establishing themselves as East End gangsters, stands on the far side of the road to the left. Violet Kray moved here in 1939 to be near her family, the Lees. Two sisters lived either side of her, and her father and brother lived across the road above their café. The

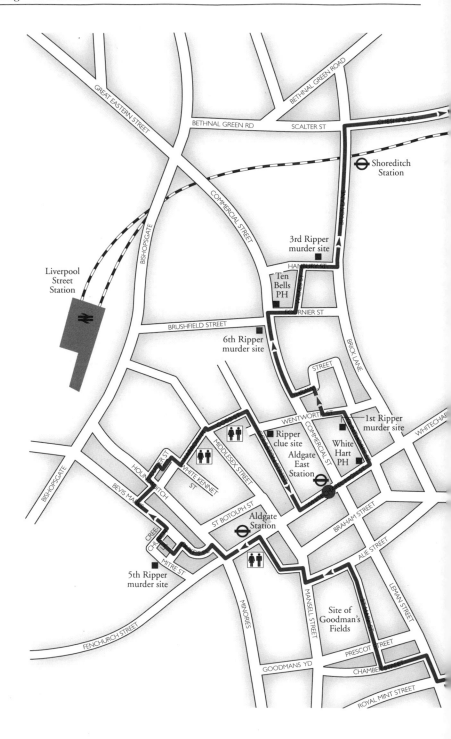

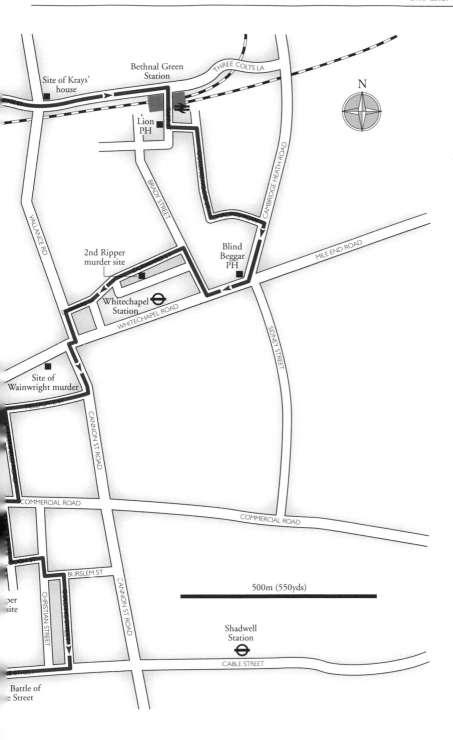

Kray twins lived at 178 until they were well into their 20s, by which time they had already made their name as villains. For Ronnie in particular the house was a haven. All he needed to be happy was to be at home with his mother, his dog, his sharp suits and his collection of swords and knives.

Cross Vallance Road and carry on along Dunbridge Street, past the garages in the railway arches. When you get to the end, turn left by the Cavalier pub into Brady Street and then right into Three Colts Street. By the entrance to Bethnal Green station turn right into Tapp Street. Beyond the railway line on the right is the Lion, a typical East End backstreets pub. Ronnie Kray was drinking here at about 8.00pm on 9 April 1966 when his spies (local boys, some of whom he slept with) brought him word that George Cornell was in the nearby Blind Beggar. Accompanied by henchman Ian Barrie and a driver, Kray went home to get his gun and then made his way to the Blind Beggar to find Cornell. (The walk passes the Blind Beggar shortly.)

Beyond the pub, follow the road round to the left and then turn first right into Collingwood Street. After a while this bends left into Darling Row, which runs into Cambridge Heath Road. On Cambridge Heath Road itself, turn right and walk down to the junction with Mile End Road (left) and Whitechapel Road (right). Straight ahead, halfway along Sidney Street on the left-hand side, is a tall block of flats with rows of balconies along the front and a partly glass-walled staircase tower to the right. Called Wexford House, this block stands on a site once occupied by several houses, including No 100, where the famous Siege of Sidney Street took place on 3 January 1911. After attempting to rob a jeweller's shop and killing three policemen in the process, two, possibly three, well armed Russian anarchists holed up in the front room on the first floor and kept not only their 400 police pursuers but also the Fire Brigade, a military force including artillery and the Home Secretary, Winston Churchill, at bay for seven hours. After a fire started mysteriously on the top floor, the house burned down. Two charred bodies were later found inside, but neither proved to be the man regarded by many as the anarchists' mastermind, the elusive, almost legendary, Peter Piatkow, better known as Peter the Painter and rumoured to have been in the house when the siege started.

Turn right into Whitechapel Road. On the right is the Blind Beggar pub, where Ronnie Kray killed George Cornell. Since the mid-1960s, when the murder took place, the interior has been modernized – probably several times – so there is little point in looking for the holes left by the two warning shots Ian Barrie fired into the ceiling as Kray strode up to his victim. Not realizing what was happening, Cornell calmly announced, 'Well, look who's here,' before Kray shot him at point-blank range. There were several onlookers, but of course nobody saw a thing – at least not until much later when Kray was safely locked away in a police cell.

Continue along Whitechapel Road past the entrance to Sainsbury's, turn right into Brady Street and then go first left into Durward Street, called Buck's Row until 1892. Walk past the new block of flats on the left to the space at the end between it and the converted school building ahead. This is the spot where Polly Nichols, believed to have been the Ripper's second victim, was found in the early hours of 31 August 1888. She was lying half in the road and half on the pavement, in front of the entrance to a stableyard between the school and a row of what were then new houses.

Walk along to the far end of Durward Road and turn left into Vallance Road. At the lights, look to the right across Whitechapel Road to a pair of tall brick gabled buildings with a date-stone saying 'AWB 1901' at the top. The one on the left (No 130) stands on the site of the warehouse where mat-and-brush-maker Henry Wainwright shot and then buried his mistress Harriet Lane on 11 September 1874. A year later, having gone bankrupt, Wainwright had to quit the warehouse, which meant he also had to get rid of the body. Dismembering it and wrapping it up in two parcels, he got someone to help him carry the parcels into the street. While Wainwright went for a cab this person peeked inside one of the parcels and was horrified to find a human hand. Wainwright then drove with the parcels across London Bridge to Southwark, where he intended to bury the remains beneath his brother's shop in Borough High Street. For the sequel to this extraordinary story see page 18.

Now cross over Whitechapel Road into New Road and take the first right into Fieldgate Street. When you get to Greenfield Street, turn left and walk down to Commercial Road. Here turn right to the lights, cross, turn left and then immediately right into Henriques Street (Berner Street in the Ripper's day). Walk on down as far as the entrance to Bernhard Baron House. The gateway almost opposite marks the approximate position of the entrance to Dutfield's Yard where Elizabeth Stride, believed to have been the Ripper's fourth victim, was found dead early on 30 September 1888. The fact that she had not been mutilated suggests that the Ripper was disturbed before he could complete his work. It also presumably explains why he was forced to kill again that same night. (The walk passes the other murder site in due course.)

At the end of Henriques Street, turn left into Fairclough Street, right into Christian Street, left into Burslem Street and right into Golding Street, formerly called Grove Street. Peter the Painter lodged at 59 Grove Street (no longer standing). When the Sidney Street anarchists were retreating from Houndsditch with their fatally wounded leader, George Gardstein, they left him to die at the Painter's house before moving on to Sidney Street for the final showdown with the authorities.

Walk under the railway line to the end of Golding Street and turn right into Cable Street. Continue along Cable Street to the lights at the junction with Dock Street/Leman Street and Royal Mint Street ahead. Here, on Sunday 4 October 1936, was fought the so-called Battle of Cable Street, a street fight between East Enders and the police prompted by British fascists' plans to march through the East End, with its large Jewish population. The fascists gathered in Royal Mint Street to begin the march; local East Enders, mobilized by communists and other left-wing groups, manned a barricade across Cable Street to stop them. The unlucky police were, as usual, caught in the middle. The battle started when the police tried to clear the route for the fascists by moving the barricade. This largely consisted of an overturned lorry full of bricks which the defenders then used as missiles against their attackers. The police failed to clear the barricade and the march was accordingly called off.

Turn right into Leman Street, go under the railway lines and turn first left into Chamber Street. Halfway along turn right into (unsigned) Magdalen Passage, which crosses the site of the 18th century Magdalen Hospital, London's first home for repentant prostitutes. Dr Dodd, the notorious clergyman hanged for forgery in 1777 (see page 145), preached the inaugural sermon at the institution's foundation in 1758 and afterwards became its official chaplain, on a salary of £100 a year.

At the end, cross Prescot Street into St Mark Street. St Mark Street cuts through what in the 18th century was open meadow known as Goodman's Fields. England's most notorious highwayman, Dick Turpin, was involved in a gun battle here in 1737 when constables tried to arrest him and his partner Robert King after they had stabled a horse stolen at Epping in a nearby inn. King was fatally wounded in the shoot-out. Turpin escaped, only to die on the gallows at York two years later.

When you get to Alie Street, turn left, cross Mansell Street, turn right and then go first left into Little Somerset Street. Follow this round to the right and into the open space (🍴) with the Still and Star pub on your right and Aldgate underground station across the road ahead. Using the lights, cross Aldgate High Street to the station and turn left. Walk round the corner in front of the church to the subway entrance (marked 'Exit 7'). Go down into the subway and come out at Exit 6 and turn right into Duke's Place. Just beyond the primary school, turn left into St James's Passage.

This leads into Mitre Square, the place where the Ripper killed for the second time on the night he was prevented from mutilating Elizabeth Stride in Berner (now Henriques) Street. The square has been completely rebuilt since the Ripper's day, but its shape and size are the same. Over in the far left-hand corner there were some vacant cottages where the flowerbeds and benches are now. It was in the corner by these cottages, early on 30 September 1888, that the Ripper murdered Catherine Eddowes, believed to have been his fifth and penultimate victim. As one ripperologist has observed, whoever the Ripper was, he was a professional: in less than 15 minutes he inveigled his victim into Mitre Square, killed her, mutilated her and made good his escape, taking her left kidney and womb with him, all virtually under the noses of four serving or ex-policeman.

Turn right along the near side of the square and exit via Mitre Passage. Turn right into Creechurch Lane and then left into Bevis Marks. After a while, take the first right into Goring Street. At its end, look across to the other side of Houndsditch. This is the site of the jewellers' shop (No 119) which the Sidney Street anarchists, encountered earlier on the walk, were attempting to rob in 1910.

Cross Houndsditch diagonally to the left and go into Cutler Street. Almost immediately turn right through the covered entrance into Clothier Street. Little more than a back yard, Clothier Street roughly covers a cul-de-sac known in 1910 as Exchange Buildings. It was from a house here that the Sidney Street anarchists were attempting to break into the rear of a jeweller's shop when they were surprised by police at 11.30pm on 16 December 1910. Opening fire, the anarchists killed three unarmed officers and seriously wounded two others before making their escape eastwards towards Sidney Street. The dead policemen were the first City officers to have been killed on duty within living memory, which says something about the state of law and order in London at that time.

Follow Clothier Street round to the left and turn right, back into Cutler Street. Then turn first left into Harrow Place. At the end (☗ on right) you come to Middlesex Street, better known as Petticoat Lane, a market street notorious historically as a recycling centre for stolen property. Cross Middlesex Street into Cobb Street (☗ on right in Leyden Street), and walk on to Bell Lane. In the early 19th century – a time when the capital's crime rate was probably higher than it has ever been before or since – No 12 Bell Lane (no longer standing) was home to 'the great Ikey Solomons', the most notorious fence in London and a major player in the Petticoat Lane property exchange. Solomon's ten-year reign ended in May 1826 when police raided his house in search of stolen watch movements. Although Solomons himself managed to escape on that occasion, his empire was effectively broken up. He was later captured and transported as a convict to Van Diemen's Land (Tasmania), where he died in 1850.

Turn right into Bell Lane and cross Wentworth Street into Goulston Street. The flats on the left stand on the site of a 19th century tenement block called Wentworth Model Dwellings. It was on the pavement outside one of the entrances to this block that the Ripper left his only known clue: a piece of Catherine Eddowes's apron, stained with her blood. The fact that it was dropped here suggests that the Ripper made his escape from Mitre Square in an easterly direction. When police discovered the apron remnant they also found a strange graffito chalked on the wall immediately above it: 'The Juwes are The Men that Will not be Blamed for nothing.' Although there was nothing to suggest that this had anything to do with the Ripper or the murders, the police feared it would fuel already prevalent rumours that the Ripper was a foreign Jew, so they hastily erased it before most people were up and about. It is possible, of course, that the Ripper also saw the graffito and deliberately dropped the piece of apron by it in order to make people think there was some connection between the murders and the Jewish community, even though there wasn't. If this was his plan it succeeded brilliantly, for ripperologists are still discussing it endlessly today.

Walk on down to the end of Goulston Street and turn left on Whitechapel High Street. Aldgate East underground station, where the walk ends, is ahead on the left.

Covent Garden and St Giles

Rookery and Red-Light District

North of the Strand, between Charing Cross Road and Drury Lane, lies the district of Covent Garden and St Giles. Covent Garden was originally a large piece of garden ground belonging to Westminster Abbey. St Giles was a medieval leper hospital which grew into the little village of St Giles in the Fields, on the main road from London to Oxford. In the 18th century Covent Garden was the centre of London's night life and a notorious red-light district – the main one in the capital. St Giles meanwhile had become a notorious slum and rookery (criminal quarter), a situation which continued well into the 19th century. By the 1840s, when the first steps were taken to clear it away, it was not just one of several notorious rookeries in London but The Rookery – its name a byword for overcrowding, disease, criminality and sheer human degradation.

Covent Garden

Dating from the early 17th century, Covent Garden and Drury Lane were originally fashionable addresses. But from the 1660s onwards new developments further west lured the nobility and gentry towards the Court, and both districts began to decline. Drury Lane went downhill rather faster than its neighbour to the west, no doubt because of its theatres. By around 1700 it had sunk so low that it had become London's main centre of prostitution. The decline of Covent Garden, already under way because of the growth of the fruit, flower and vegetable market in the centre of the square, speeded up in the 1720s and 1730s when the square's owners started letting houses as taverns, coffee houses and bagnios and when the Covent Garden Theatre opened in 1732. Not surprisingly, by 1750 the last titled tenants had left Covent Garden forever. The Garden then entered its heyday as the premier red-light district in London. From late evening until early in the morning the place was positively crawling with prostitutes. As local magistrate Sir John Fielding said in 1776: 'One would imagine that all the prostitutes in the kingdom had picked upon this blessed neighbourhood for a place of general rendezvous.'

Certain taverns, coffee houses, bagnios and brothels enjoyed a particular notoriety as places for meeting and sleeping with prostitutes. First of all there was Tom King's Coffee-House. This was in one of the wooden market buildings on the south side of the square. Tom was a well-bred Eton and Cambridge dropout who had married a local Covent Garden girl and started a coffee house at some time in the late 1720s. Thanks to his social connections — and to the attractions of a black waitress called Tawny Betty — it was a popular haunt for upper-class rakes. Although plenty of prostitutes also patronized Tom's, it was a house of assignation only: there were no beds on the premises, so gentlemen wishing to consummate were obliged to take their companions elsewhere, perhaps to the woman's lodging or to a tavern or bagnio where it was possible to hire private rooms.

Overlooking Tom King's Coffee-House from Tavistock Row on the south side of the square, was Mother Douglas's brothel. This had actually been started in the early 1730s by the famous Betsy Careless, after she had lost the charms that had once made her the most celebrated courtesan of her day. But Betsy was no businesswoman; also, she was rather too fond of the bottle. In 1735 she was evicted. In 1739 Jane Douglas took over Betsy's business, and for the next twenty years she dominated the brothel business in Covent Garden. Mother Douglas died in 1761, having earned immortality through the hand of artist and former Covent Garden resident William Hogarth, who depicted her in no fewer than three of his pictures.

Just round the corner from Mother Douglas's brothel, in a section of the square known as the Little Piazza, was a bagnio known as the Hummums. 'Bagnio' (Italian) and 'hummums' (Arabic) were actually interchangeable terms for warm baths, or, as we would call them, Turkish baths. Turkish baths were introduced to England in 1678 and to Covent Garden (the walk passes the site of the first) in 1682. Before long they were all over the capital, but the highest concentration was in Covent Garden where, besides bathing, sweating and cupping (blood-letting), they also offered overnight accommodation. Many allowed men and women to sleep together, and so were ideal for men who could not take girls home to their lodgings. The 44-year-old Virginian landowner William Byrd, in London on business in 1718 and 1719, records many occasions in his diary when he slept all night with women at the bagnio in Silver Street (now covered by the east end of New Oxford Street). On 16 June 1718, for example, having dined with Annie Wilkinson at the Union tavern in Long Acre, he took her to the Silver Street bagnio 'where I lay all night with her and rogered her three times and found her very straight and unprecocious and very sweet and agreeable'. Annie subsequently became Mr Byrd's laundress.

The Hummums in the Little Piazza was run by a Mrs Gould, and appears to have doubled up as a brothel. Her clientele consisted of merchants, bankers and brokers from the City who, under pretence of going into the country for the weekend, came instead to her establishment and spent from Saturday until Monday enjoying fine food and wine and the charms of the better class of prostitutes. These cost as much as several guineas. Streetwalkers at this time charged as little as 2s 6d for a quick turn in the park or up some dark alley.

The two most notorious taverns in the area were the Rose and the Shakespeare's Head. The Rose was close to the Drury Lane Theatre and derived much of its trade from that establishment. Apparently it was also famous for its 'posture girls', the 18th century term for strippers. The Shakespeare's Head was in the northeast corner of Covent Garden, next door to the entrance to the Covent Garden Theatre (forerunner of today's Royal Opera House). In the 1740s the head waiter, Jack Harris, began compiling for his customers a list of girls, later printed as *Harris's List of Covent Garden Ladies*, the earliest known copies of which date from the late 1750s. *Harris's List* was the public face of a substantial pimping empire which apparently had close links with Mrs Douglas's brothel across the square. In 1759 both Harris and Mrs Douglas were charged with procuring girls. In a published defence, Harris admitted that he was a pimp, but boasted that it was thanks to him and his London-wide network of agents constantly searching for new faces among serving maids and apprentice milliners that there was, as he put it, 'such a fine nursery of whores particularly fresh in the town'. Harris died in 1766, but an enterprising publisher carried on producing new editions of his list until the 1790s.

One of the Shakespeare's Head's most famous customers was that well known rake and biographer James Boswell. Boswell, who lost his virginity in Covent Garden when he was 19 (the walk passes the site), no doubt visited the Shakespeare's Head when he was wooing Louisa Lewis, the 'handsome actress' from Covent Garden Theatre whom he bedded at the Black Lion Inn in Water Lane, Temple (see page 32). A few months after that conquest – on the evening of 19 May 1763, three days following his first meeting with Dr Johnson – he met two girls in the arcade outside the Shakespeare's Head, took them into a private room along with a bottle of sherry,

> and then solaced my existence with them, one
> after the other, according to their seniority. I was
> quite raised, as the phrase is: thought I was in a
> London tavern, the Shakespeare's Head, enjoying
> high debauchery after my sober winter. I parted

> with my ladies politely and came home in a glow
> of spirits.

Boswell later discovered that one of the girls had given him gonorrhoea. In the same year, 1763, William Hickey discovered the delights of Covent Garden as a 14-year-old bunking off from Westminster School. Like Boswell, he lost his virginity in the Garden. It happened when he was walking in the arcade outside the Shakespeare's Head and 'a very pretty little girl, apparently not much older than myself' accosted him. She said: 'You are a very handsome boy and too young to be walking in such a place as this alone. Come home with me and I'll take your maidenhead.' Hickey, not one to look a gift horse in the mouth, went with her:

> to a very indifferent-looking apartment up three pair
> of stairs in a dark, narrow court out of Drury Lane.
> There we took off our clothes and got into a dirty,
> miserable bed. My companion gave me great credit
> for my vigour, saying I was a famous little fellow, and
> should prove an invaluable acquisition to whatever
> girl was lucky enough to fix me. In this den of
> wretchedness I passed three truly happy hours.

Having left school and started work as an articled clerk in a lawyer's office, Hickey took to supping with a group of friends at a coffee house in St Martin's Lane and then adjourning at about 11.00pm to Bow Street, 'in which street there were then three most notorious bawdy houses', one of which was right next door to the house of Sir John Fielding, the local magistrate. In these brothels, which they visited in rotation, Hickey and his friends usually spent three to four hours drinking punch and romping with the girls before pairing off with their chosen companions for sex, usually in the girls' lodgings. Though the brothels were 'low and infamous', Hickey nevertheless met with some 'very beautiful women' in them. And Mother Hamilton, the madam of one of the brothels, always let him know whenever she had in a 'particularly smart or handsome new piece'. When he was 19, Hickey was taken away by his father from the fleshpots of London and sent out to India, but before he left Hickey hosted a dinner at the Shakespeare's Head in December 1768 at which the principal guests were his favourite Covent Garden whore and a few of her prostitute friends.

Covent Garden continued to be a notorious red-light district long after Hickey's time, but by the end of the 18th century the prostitutes had begun to move westwards in the wake of their male clientele.

St Giles

While young gentlemen like Hickey and Boswell were sowing their wild oats in Covent Garden, thousands of people were living just a few streets away in St Giles in conditions of abject misery and squalor.

St Giles was developed in the 17th century, like Covent Garden and Drury Lane, but it never shared their high social status. For some reason — possibly because it was said to have been built on marshy ground (the marsh being the reason for the pronounced southward curve in St Giles High Street) — it had a higher than usual proportion of poor families. In the second half of the 17th century the development of the West End lured the better-off away, leaving many houses empty and decaying. These gradually filled up with a population of casual labourers, street hawkers, beggars, tramps, thieves and prostitutes. Some were permanent residents, but many were transients attracted by the cheap lodging houses, where beds were available for as little as 2d a night. A significant proportion — possibly the majority of St Giles's population — consisted of poor Irish immigrants. In fact, ever since the 17th century St Giles had been something of an Irish colony.

The gin craze of the 1720s–50s hit St Giles hard. Every fourth house was a gin shop, and the 82 lodging houses in the area retailed the stuff too. Like drugs today, cheap, addictive, poisonous gin wrecked lives and led to much crime and misery. One hopes the tragic case of the woman who killed her child in order to sell its clothes to buy gin was an exception, but one fears it was not. Legislation in 1751 ended the gin scandal, which had well-nigh ruined not just St Giles but all London. William Hogarth's satirical print *Gin Lane* played a part in securing this legislation. There never was a Gin Lane in London, but the presence of St George's Bloomsbury in the background of Hogarth's picture shows that he had St Giles in mind when he drew it.

In the 19th century, gross overcrowding led to a worsening of conditions in St Giles. It was at this time that it became known as the most notorious rookery in the whole of London (the use of the word 'rookery' in this context first appears in 1829). A rookery was regarded not just as a slum but as a criminals' quarter, where professional criminals lived and brought up their children to follow in their footsteps. In St Giles, as in other rookeries, boys were taught to be pickpockets and girls to be prostitutes. Lodging-house keepers like the notorious Mother Cummings of 6 George Street (now Dyott Street) were at the heart of the problem. In addition to her primary function, she was also a fence for stolen property, a bawdy-house keeper and a trainer of young criminals. In particular she employed young prostitutes to lure drunken men to her house and then rob them. The children of St Giles stood little chance in life, hence the saying that 'St Giles breed/Better hang than seed'.

In 1816 there was said to be a fluctuating Irish population in the rookery of about 6000 adults and 3–4000 children. They were crammed into every available space, from cellars right up to the garrets. Cellar dwellings, entered via trap-doors in the pavement, were a particular feature of St Giles and Seven Dials. Whole families, sometimes groups of families, lived and worked (together with animals in some cases) in these dark, dank, dismal holes where running water and sanitation were unheard-of luxuries. A 'St Giles cellar' became proverbial for the very lowest class of accommodation.

Many 19th century visitors to St Giles were appalled at what they found. Frederick Engels, Karl Marx's collaborator, published this description in 1844:

> The houses are occupied from cellar to garret, filthy within and without, and their appearance is such that no human being could possibly wish to live in them. But all this is nothing in comparison with the dwellings in the narrow courts and alleys between the streets, entered by covered passages between the houses, in which the filth and tottering ruin surpass all description. Scarcely a whole window-pane can be found, the walls are crumbling, door-posts and window-frames loose and broken, doors of old boards nailed together, or altogether wanting in this thieves' quarter, where no doors are needed, there being nothing to steal. Heaps of garbage and ashes lie in all directions, and the foul liquids emptied before the doors gather in stinking pools. Here live the poorest of the poor, the worst paid workers with thieves and the victims of prostitution indiscriminately huddled together, the majority Irish, or of Irish extraction, and those who have not yet sunk in the whirlpool of moral ruin which surrounds them, sinking daily deeper, losing daily more and more of their power to resist the demoralizing influence of want, filth, and evil surroundings.

The beginning of the end for St Giles came in 1840 when, to relieve congestion in St Giles High Street, a new road was authorized to connect Oxford Street and Holborn. Completed in 1847, New Oxford Street required the demolition of over 250 houses. The Duke of Bedford, the owner of 104 of them, received £114,000 in compensation. The 5000 inhabitants were simply evicted. Left to shift for themselves, they crowded into surrounding streets – like Church Lane, for example, where the average house occupancy jumped from 21 to 40. In 1849, as many as 90 people were sleeping at night in some houses, though by this time refugees from the famine in Ireland were also contributing to the problem. The St Giles rookery was not eventually destroyed until the 1880s, by which time Church Lane had been torn down and Shaftesbury Avenue and Charing Cross Road had been built.

THE COVENT GARDEN WALK

Start and finish: Covent Garden underground station (Piccadilly line).
Length: 1¾ miles (2.8km).
Refreshments: Places of all kinds to eat and drink abound in and around Covent Garden at the start and finish of the walk. By comparison the St Giles area at the midway stage is a desert. The well-heeled might like to note that in its early stages the walk passes Rule's in Maiden Lane, a famous restaurant claimed to be the oldest in London.

After coming out of Covent Garden station, turn left and then left again into Long Acre. Continue along this street. After a while you reach a sign pointing into Banbury Court on the left (it's roughly opposite Mercer Street on the right). This is the approximate site of the Duke's Bagnio, opened in 1682, one of the earliest Turkish baths in London and the first in Covent Garden. Covent Garden subsequently became notorious for its bagnios, many of which allowed men to stay all night with prostitutes in private rooms. Whether the Duke's Bagnio was one of these establishments is not known for sure. What is known about the Duke's is that, on 14 November 1712, the rake Lord Mohun, one of the most belligerent duellists of his time, spent the night here before going to Hyde Park for an early-morning encounter with the Duke of Hamilton. Both the principals were killed. The seconds, who also fought, survived.

Carry on along Long Acre. Towards the end look out for the black door on the right at 136-7 Long Acre; it has an arch above it and, above the arch, a relief bust of a woman. This is the site of the house of 17th century poet John Dryden, of whom more in a minute.

Opposite 136-7, turn left into the covered entrance of Rose Street. Turn left on Floral Street and then first right into Lazenby Court. The passage brings you back into Rose Street in front of the Lamb and Flag pub. On the night of 18 December 1679 Dryden was returning home when he was attacked somewhere about here by three men, who 'calling him rogue and son of a whore knocked him down and dangerously wounded him, but upon his crying out murther they made their escape'. Royal favourite and fellow poet the Earl of Rochester is thought to have ordered the beating in revenge for some insulting lines in a poem which he (wrongly) believed Dryden to have written. 'Mean in every action, lewd in every limb' is the sort of thing to which Rochester not unreasonably took exception. The painted board on the roof of the passage by the pub refers to the incident.

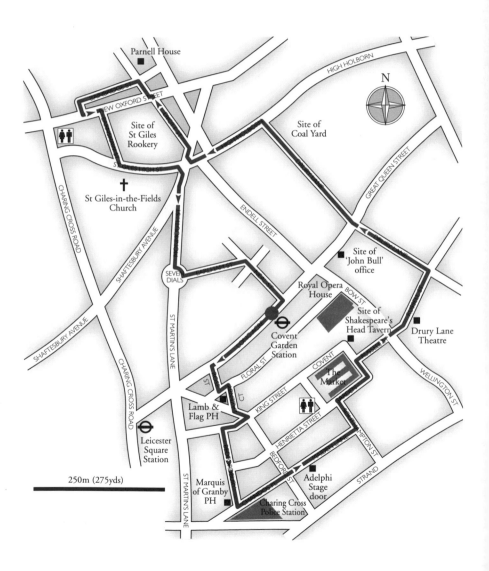

Now carry on down Rose Street to Garrick Street. Turn left here, right into New Row and left again into Bedfordbury. At the far end, on the right, the Marquis of Granby is supposed to be the descendant of the Hole in the Wall, the 17th century pub where highwayman Claude Duval was finally tracked down and arrested while drunk. One of the most notorious moonlight marauders of his day, he was famed not just for his daring exploits but also for his sympathetic, not to say romantic, treatment of female victims. His chivalry did not save him, however, because he was convicted at the Old Bailey and hanged at Tyburn on Friday 21 January 1670. After his corpse had been cut down, it lay in state at the Tangier Tavern in St Giles, attracting huge crowds. Opinions differ as to whether he is buried in Covent Garden Church or St Giles: Covent Garden has a memorial stone but no entry in the burial register; St Giles has no stone, but it does have a Duval entry in the burial register, dated the day after the lying-in-state. This would clinch the argument were it not for the fact that the entry relates to a Peter Duval, not a Claude!

Now turn left into Chandos Place. On the right-hand side here used to be in the 18th century a little street called Vine Street. Franz Kotzwara, a popular composer in England and America, died in Vine Street in prostitute Susannah Hill's room about 3.00pm on Friday 2 September 1791. The precise details of what happened are not known – the judge at Susannah's murder trial ordered all reports of the case to be destroyed in the interests of public decency – but it seems he was into auto-erotic asphyxiation and somehow managed to hang himself from a doorknob. Apparently he had earlier asked Susannah to mutilate him by cutting off his penis. Clearly he was in an extremely disturbed state of mind, so it is not surprising Susannah was acquitted of his murder.

Continue along Chandos Street, past Agar Street on the right. When you get to Bedford Street, look right into the bottom section, which leads into the Strand. In the 18th century, when this was called Half Moon Street, a Mrs Phillips had a shop here, seven doors from the Strand on the right-hand side, where she sold condoms. Apparently Mother Douglas, the leading Covent Garden madam of the day, used to buy them wholesale. The Phillips shop was one of at least two places in the Covent Garden area where it was possible to obtain condoms; the other was J. Jacobs in Oliver's Alley, a cul-de-sac entered from the Strand a little way east of where you are standing now. First introduced into England around the 1670s, condoms at this date were cumbersome articles made of sheep gut and tied on with a piece of coloured ribbon. They were expensive, and so only the better-off used them, and they were mainly employed to avoid disease rather than to prevent conception. Boswell called them his armour.

Continue straight on into Maiden Lane. Just beyond Exchange Court on the right is the stage door of the Adelphi Theatre (main entrance in the Strand). As the plaque on the wall indicates, this is the spot where William Terris, one of the leading actors of his day and hero of the so-called Adelphi melodramas, met his end on 16 December 1897. He was just entering the theatre for his nightly performance when Richard Prince, an impecunious and unknown actor maddened by jealousy, stepped out from the shadows on the other side of the street and stabbed him three times. Terris died half an hour later. Prince, known to many as Mad Archie, was judged to be insane and ended his days in Broadmoor.

Further along Maiden Lane on the left is Rule's, founded in 1798 and supposed to be the oldest restaurant in London. In a curtained alcove on the first floor, that great womanizer Bertie, Prince of Wales, Queen Victoria's eldest son and later Edward VII, wined and dined actress Lily Langtry (see page 133).

At the end of Maiden Lane you come to Southampton Street. It was at the Blue Periwig tavern here that James Boswell, wild-oat-sower and biographer-to-be of Dr Johnson, lost his virginity to noted whore Sally Forrester in May 1760, when he was 19. In typically high-flown style, Boswell subsequently pointed out the tavern to friends as 'the house in which I first paid my addresses to the Paphian Queen [i.e., Venus], where I first experienced the melting and transporting rites of love'.

Now turn left into Southampton Street, walk up to Covent Garden (🚻 left beside St Paul's Church, where Claude Duval is supposedly buried) and turn right. In the early 18th century the market in Covent Garden consisted of a row of wooden buildings where the arcade on the left is (there is a tile picture of the early market in the Gents and maybe in the Ladies too). Tom King's Coffee-House occupied one of these buildings. On the right there was a terrace of houses called Tavistock Row: Mother Douglas's brothel was one of these. Mrs Gould's bagnio–brothel, the Hummums, was directly ahead, where the London Transport Museum is now.

Walk on to the end of the market building and turn left up the east side as far as the entrance to Russell Street on the right. In the top right (northeast) corner of the square a modern arcade has replaced the original one, called the Piazza. The entrance to Covent Garden Theatre, opened in 1732, was in the corner. It was in this theatre (now the Royal Opera House) that George Barrington, the so-called 'prince of pickpockets' and one of the most celebrated criminals of the 18th century, stole a snuffbox said to be worth £30,000 from the Russian Prince Orloff. Luckily for Barrington, the Prince declined to prosecute. Much later, however, Barrington was convicted of other crimes and transported to Australia, where he spent the rest of his life.

To the right of the theatre, under the colonnade, was the Shakespeare's Head, where in 1763 Boswell 'solaced his existence' with two prostitutes – for free, which must have pleased him. That same year the Shakespeare's Head was honoured with a visit from Casanova. Having been recommended to the tavern by another notorious rake, Lord Pembroke, Casanova turned up one night, took a private room and asked the landlord to find him a pretty girl to dine with. Girl after girl was presented, but none took the great lover's fancy. Eventually Casanova realized the landlord's pimp was making sport of him for the sake of the shilling he generously gave each rejected girl. 'That is very probable,' said the landlord. 'It often happens when a gentleman does not choose a girl who is on the list [i.e., *Harris's List of Covent Garden Ladies*].'

To the right of the Shakespeare's Head was the Bedford Coffee House. On the evening of 7 April 1779 the Reverend James Hackman sat here having a drink. When people started coming out of the theatre at the end of the play he approached one of them – Martha Ray – as she was being handed into her carriage and shot her in the head. He turned a second pistol on himself but it either missed or misfired. He was arrested, tried for murder and executed at Tyburn. Hackman had loved Martha for years but had been unable to woo her away from her long-standing lover and the father of her children, the Cabinet Minister Lord Sandwich. It's thought his original plan was to shoot himself in front of her, but in a moment of vengeful madness he suddenly decided to take her life as well as his own.

Now turn right into Russell Street. At the first corner on the left was Will's Coffee House, the most famous of many similar establishments in the Covent Garden of the late 17th/early 18th centuries. It was from here that Dryden was returning home when he was beaten up in 1679. In 1718–19 William Byrd visited it most evenings to play cards or read the papers, and, in 1719 at least, to wait for his then mistress, Mrs Betty S–t–r–d. Several times in January, February and March of that year she picked him up here around 10.00 pm and they then went to a bagnio for sex. On 20 January he 'rogered her three times with vigour'; on 29 January four times; on 17 February twice; and on 5 March 'but once'.

Cross the entrance to Bow Street (where William Hickey regularly visited three brothels in the 1760s) and continue on to the arcade beside the Drury Lane Theatre. Here, when the theatre was much smaller, was the Rose tavern, notorious for its 'posture girls' (strippers). The tavern was demolished when the theatre was enlarged in 1766. Drury Lane actresses have provided several royal mistresses, including Nell Gwynn (Charles II), Perdita Robinson (George IV) and Mrs Jordan (William IV). The theatre has also been the scene of two attempted royal assassinations: in 1716 on the future George II and in 1800 on George III.

Continue along to the end of the theatre arcade and turn left into Drury Lane, the centre of London's prostitution trade around 1700. By that time the large houses that lined this once-fashionable street had been split up into tenements and their grounds covered with a dense mass of courts and alleyways – at least 27 between Long Acre to the north and the Strand to the south. A couple – Martlett Court and Broad Court – survive on the left, although all the old housing here has long since been replaced by large blocks of council flats. Prostitution survived in and around Drury Lane long after the main centre of the trade had moved west, first to Covent Garden and then in the 19th century to Haymarket and the West End.

Carry on along Drury Lane. The Great Plague of 1665 first appeared in this area, which says something about its condition at the time. On 7 June that year Pepys was in Drury Lane and saw for the first time the tell-tale red crosses on front doors indicating the presence of the contagion.

Cross the junction of Long Acre and Great Queen Street. Towards the far end of Drury Lane you come to Macklin Street, on the right. Once known as Lewknor Lane, this was one of the most notorious streets in London in the 18th century. If St Giles was a byword for poverty and crime, Lewknor Lane was a byword for loose living. One writer said it 'swarmed with notoriously lascivious and profligate strumpets'. Some apparently were common tarts while others were more high-class, like Letitia Smith, mistress first of highwayman Sixteen-String Jack (real name Jack Rann) and then of the Duke of York. Letitia eventually married Sir John Lade. Her sister's daughter married the 7th Earl of Barrymore, a notorious rake, in 1792. He was killed the following year when his gun went off accidentally; she became an alcoholic and decades later, in 1832, died alone in Charles Court, Drury Lane, with no more than twopence-halfpenny and an empty gin bottle to her name. Nobody claimed her body, so it was sent to King's College Hospital for dissection.

Just beyond Macklin Street you come to Stukeley Street, known as the Coal Yard when Nell Gwynn – orange-seller, Drury Lane actress and mistress of Charles II (see pages 127 and 137) – was born here in 1650. At the end of Drury Lane turn left into High Holborn and walk along to the junction with Endell Street; the main road continues as St Giles High Street. Built in the 1840s, Endell Street covers the site of the Bowl, the St Giles inn where condemned prisoners on their way from Newgate gaol to the gallows at Tyburn stopped for a last drink (see page 29). After the clearance of the St Giles rookery a school, a public bath and wash-house and a parish workhouse were all built in Endell Street as part of the Victorians' attempts to improve the lot of the desperately poor and deprived local population. The Oasis sports centre and swimming pool on the corner beside you stands on the site of the public bath and wash-house. The workhouse, behind the wash-house, was demolished in the 1970s. The former school building still stands opposite the Oasis on the other side of Endell Street.

Now cross Endell Street, turn right across St Giles High Street at the lights and carry on into Dyott Street. You are now entering what was once the St Giles rookery, the most notorious of several similar areas in 19th century London, although Jacob's Island in Bermondsey and Saffron Hill, north of Holborn (see page 36), were almost on a par with it. Dickens described them all at one stage or another, covering St Giles in *Sketches by Boz* (1836). Dyott Street was the main street of the St Giles rookery. Mother Cummings's lodging house was here, and so was the Rat's Castle, the most infamous tavern in the area. It was in a Dyott Street tavern − perhaps the Rat's Castle − that highwaymen Owen Haggerty and John Holloway planned some of their crimes, including a murder on Hounslow Heath. When they were executed outside Newgate gaol in 1807 the crowd of 40,000 stampeded, killing 28 and seriously injuring 70 (see page 30).

William Hare, arguably the worse half of the notorious bodysnatching duo Burke and Hare, ended his days as a beggar in the St Giles slums. Having turned King's Evidence against Burke, who was hanged in Edinburgh in 1829 (see page 19), he was smuggled out of Scotland to England. He worked for a time at a lime works in the Midlands, but when his workmates found out who he was they threw lime in his face and blinded him. Hare then came to St Giles, making a living by begging with a metal plate in the streets around New Oxford Street and the British Museum. His only companions were a guide-dog and a woman who joined him at the end of each day. In his autobiography lawyer William Ballantine says he often saw them meet in his youth but 'never noticed a smile on the face of either of them'.

When you get to New Oxford Street, the new road driven through the heart of the rookery in 1847, use the lights to cross to the right and continue into the northern section of Dyott Street. When New Oxford Street was built, nothing was done officially to provide alternative homes for the thousands of people evicted to make way for it, but the Society for Improving the Conditions of the Working Classes did make a contribution in the form of a block of 54 model flats, each with its own living room, two bedrooms, scullery and water closet. Now called Parnell House and part of the Peabody Trust, this building survives at the corner of Streatham Street and Dyott Street and is the oldest building of its kind in London. Note the words 'Model Homes for Families' in the string course above the Streatham Street entrance.

From the junction with Streatham Street you can see Great Russell Street ahead. This was the northern limit of the rookery. Now turn left into Bainbridge Street. This takes you back to New Oxford Street (⊞ right in St Giles Circus subway). Turn left here and then cross right into Earnshaw Street; part of this street covers Church Lane, the last part of the rookery to be cleared in the late 1870s.

Earnshaw Street brings you back to St Giles High Street. Opposite is the parish church, originally the chapel of the leper hospital and later the nucleus of the little village of St Giles. Here is buried the Countess of Shrewsbury. In a notoriously immoral age Pepys – no saint himself – called her a 'whore', but she really owes her notoriety to the story that, when her lover, the Duke of Buckingham, fought a duel over her with her husband, the Earl of Shrewsbury, in January 1668, she was present disguised as a page and armed with pistols with which she intended to shoot both herself and her husband if her lover were killed. The truth of the matter is that she was living in a French convent at the time. Both lover and husband survived.

Now cross St Giles High Street and turn left. When you get to Shaftesbury Avenue turn right. Cross left over the zebra crossing and turn right into Monmouth Street. This takes you down to Seven Dials, a small circus with six streets radiating off it and a central column doubling as a sundial. Like St Giles, Seven Dials was a rough area almost from the time it was built in the late 1600s. In 1773 the recently replaced central column was removed, partly because it was thought a horde of treasure was buried underneath and partly because it had become a focal point for thieves and beggars. Much of their loot no doubt resurfaced in Monmouth Street, which was a seedy emporium of second-hand goods, particularly clothes and shoes, until well into the 19th century.

Leave Seven Dials via Earlham Street (next to the Cambridge Theatre). At the end of Earlham Street turn right into Neal Street. Cross Shelton Street and continue up to Long Acre. On your left now a modern development of shops and flats covers the site of Odham's printing works, started in Floral Street in 1894 and moved here in 1906. Odham's printed the notorious Horatio Bottomley's *John Bull* magazine (see page 46), whose offices were at 67 Long Acre (further along to your left, beyond the roundabout). When Bottomley failed to pay his printing bills – surprise, surprise – Odham's, whose prosperity was based on the swindler's big-selling magazine (its peak circulation was a massive 1.7 million), bought the title and published it themselves.

Across the road from the Odham's site is Covent Garden station, where the walk ends.

Plate 18: *The Blind Beggar pub on the corner of Whitechapel Road and Cambridge Heath Road where gangster Ronnie Kray shot George Cornell in 1966 (see pages 64 and 70, and plate 20).*

Plate 19: *The Kray twins (Reggie left and Ronnie right) dominated London's underworld in the 1960s (see the East End chapter).*

Plate 20: *George Cornell, shot dead by Ronnie Kray in the Blind Beggar pub (see pages 64 and 70, and plate 18).*

Plate 21: *A bomb - believed to have been the IRA's – wrecked this bus in Aldwych in 1996 (see page 98).* Plate 22: *Gin Lane (1750-1):William Hogarth's political print is thought to be based on the notorious slum of St Giles (see page 79).*

Plate 23: In its former guise as a variety theatre, the Empire cinema, Leicester Square, was a notorious haunt of prostitutes (see page 105). Plate 24: Modern Soho's sex trade is based in and around Walker's Court, home of the Raymond Revuebar (see pages 110 and 116).

Plate 25: *Sir Edmund Berry Godfrey's death in 1678 is a notorious murder mystery (see page 102).*

Plate 26: *Two Soho 'models' soliciting from their first-floor rooms in the 1950s (see page 106).*

Plate 27: *One of the infamous Messina family on his way to deportation in 1959 (see page 107).*

Strand and Haymarket
Victorian Prostitution

In the 18th century, when neighbouring Covent Garden was London's main red-light district, streetwalkers (i.e., prostitutes who solicited in the streets) were common in the Strand. James Boswell records being accosted by one in July 1763 when he was walking with Dr Johnson. 'No, no, my girl,' said Johnson kindly. 'It won't do.' Boswell and Johnson then talked of 'the wretched life of such women, and agreed that much more misery than happiness, upon the whole, is produced by illicit commerce between the sexes'. The hypocrite Boswell, however, was saying one thing and practising another. As his diary shows, he was a regular customer of London's prostitutes at this time, and on several occasions picked up his whores in the Strand. Just a few weeks before his nocturnal stroll with Dr Johnson, he 'picked up a little profligate wench' in the Strand 'and gave her sixpence. She allowed me entrance. But the miscreant refused me performance. I was much stronger than her, and volens nolens pushed her up against the wall.' The girl wriggled away from him and escaped. Perhaps she was frightened by the size of his member; on a previous occasion another Strand prostitute had 'wondered' at it and told Boswell that 'if I ever took a girl's maidenhead, I would make her squeak'.

In Boswell's time, though, it was really Covent Garden that was notorious for its prostitutes. A century later that notoriety had shifted to the Strand and to the broad north–south street on the other side of Trafalgar Square, the Haymarket. The reason for the shift was the theatres. After 1843, when controls on theatres were removed, there was an explosion of theatre-building both in the Strand, which was one of the capital's busiest thoroughfares and therefore an ideal location, and in the Haymarket, which was already home to an old-established theatre and the capital's opera house. Theatres always attracted prostitution. So it was in Shakespeare's Bankside (see chapter 1), so it was in 18th century Drury Lane and Covent Garden (see chapter 5), and so it was in the 19th century Strand and Haymarket. Only this time, because of the profusion of theatres, music halls and other places of entertainment, and the consequent huge number of potential customers, the prostitution was on a far, far bigger scale and therefore more conspicuous and outrageous than it had ever been before.

By day London's street prostitutes did most of their business in the main middle-class shopping districts of Bond Street, Regent Street and Oxford Street. But, as the afternoon wore on, the street market in prostitution gradually drifted south to the theatre district of the Strand and the Haymarket. By around 3.00pm or 4.00pm, so it was said, there were already so many prostitutes here that it was impossible for a respectable woman to walk from the top of Haymarket to the Wellington Street end of the Strand. By 7.00pm the Strand was 'literally impassable' to both men and women, and it remained so until the early hours of the morning, by which time the last revellers were departing to their beds.

Any man walking along the Strand at this time could rely on being accosted by a prostitute at almost every step. In the early part of the evening the girls were relatively modest and polite but, as the night wore on and the drink took effect, they became more and more insistent, even rude. Some of the prostitutes were dress-harlots, whores who rented fine clothes and false hair to make themselves more attractive. The owners of these trappings – usually hard-bitten old women operating from Catherine Street, between the Strand and Covent Garden – arranged for the girls, whom they treated as virtual slaves, to be followed as they patrolled their beats to ensure they did not run off with the valuable property.

Many of the prostitutes were very young. The Russian novelist Dostoevsky, who spent eight days in London and was appalled at the horrific scenes he witnessed, particularly in the Haymarket, observed mothers bringing their daughters to solicit. 'Little girls aged about twelve seize you by the arms and beg you to come with them.'

Sex was performed in short-term hotels and rented rooms. Throughout the area, shops and more or less respectable-looking houses displayed notices saying 'Beds to Let'. 'At evening,' recalled French writer Hippolyte Taine,

> numerous figures are to be seen entering and leaving, figures which have the bearing, the look, the gravity which is peculiarly English. The mature man, the young man of the respectable classes – on this evening he is supposed to be travelling or at his club. He does not make himself conspicuous, does not offer his companion his arm: his expedition is secret and anonymous and represents no more than an escape of the beast which everyone of us carries within himself.

Besides the street, prostitutes solicited in the generously-proportioned promenades of theatres and music halls, in the massive dancing saloons and in certain restaurants where they were welcomed because they attracted male customers.

The heyday of this superficially glittering world of debauchery and dissipation was the 1860s, and the centre of it was undoubtedly the Haymarket – 'the street of midnight adventure', as one contemporary called it; 'the centre of the surging mass of nocturnal corruption', according to another.

By day there was nothing peculiar about the Haymarket, except perhaps for the unusually large number of gin palaces, hotels, French restaurants, oyster shops, Turkish dewans, lounges, cafés and coffee houses with their blinds drawn. On the west side there were even a few respectable shops, although most honest tradesmen had been driven out during the 1850s. In the year 1858 alone 137 shops and other business premises had been converted into various kinds of night-houses (precursors of the modern night-club).

By night, when these night-houses opened their doors, the Haymarket was completely transformed. The eating and drinking establishments, vulgarly furnished with bright lights, mirrors, gilt and red plush, were alive with people, laughter and music. Outside, under the flaring gas lamps, crowds of people surged along the wide pavements, from the arcades round Her Majesty's Theatre right up the street and across Piccadilly to the Quadrant (the south end of Regent Street). There were all types: elegant top-hatted gentlemen still clutching their opera glasses from the theatre, prostitutes in their finery and shadowed by their bullies (protectors), tramps, beggars and street vendors, and everywhere children, shoeless, dirty, dressed in rags and all too frequently alone.

Towards midnight the pace picked up as the theatres, music halls and dancing saloons began to disgorge their customers. Those men who had been excited by titillating shows and troupes of scantily clad dancing girls were easy meat for the hordes of prostitutes thronging the street and the theatre entrances. It was now that the night-houses – all-night drinking establishments catering for prostitutes and their clients after the theatres, music halls and dance halls had closed – came into their own. Strictly speaking, they were not permitted to serve alcohol or allow dancing, but there was little to stop them. Police raids did take place, but not in such a way as to inconvenience anybody. One old roué recalled that, as soon as the police knocked at the door and the alarm was given, 'carpets were turned up in the twinkling of an eye, boards were raised, and glasses and bottles – empty or full – were thrust promiscuously in. Everyone assumed a virtuous air and talked in subdued tones.' If there were any musicians, which there usually were, they were hastily thrust in a cupboard or empty room. Then 'a bevy of police, headed by an inspector, marched solemnly in, and having completed the farce, marched solemnly out'. Of course, many police of the time – including most probably these ones – were on the take.

The two most notorious Haymarket establishments were the Argyll Rooms and Kate Hamilton's. Neither was actually in the street, but they were both close by and they were prominent features of the nocturnal landscape of the Haymarket district.

The Argyll was a dancing saloon in Great Windmill Street, just north of Haymarket. Founded by wine merchant Robert Bignell and open by 1851, it had a huge, double-height room 116ft (35.3m) long. A gallery ran round all four sides, with musicians seated at one end. Behind them a large gilt-framed mirror reflected the whole length of the hall. Below, long benches for the dancers lined the walls, which were hung with large gilt-framed pictures and mirrors. Massive gasoliers suspended from the ceiling cast a brilliant glaring light over the crowded dance floor.

As the Haymarket scene developed, the Argyll became notorious as a promenade for the better class of prostitutes, so forcing up rents in surrounding streets. At the Argyll could be seen all the best-known professional courtesans – the demi-reps or demi-mondaines, as they were called – of the day. The one most closely associated with the Argyll was Cora Pearl, one of the 19th century's most outrageous courtesans. Having been seduced as a young girl by an elderly man and therefore, in the eyes of Victorian society, 'ruined', she began her career at the Argyll, where she soon attracted the attention of the proprietor, by now grown wealthy on the proceeds of his enterprise. Bignell took her to Paris but, unluckily for him, she did not return with him, instead becoming the toast of more liberated French high society and acquiring a string of royal and aristocratic lovers – notably the emperor's cousin, Prince Napoleon – together with a large house and an equally impressive retinue of servants. But her looks were her fortune: when one went, so did the other. Cora died in poverty in Paris in 1886, aged about 50.

Having tumbled out of the Argyll with his chosen companion, a man on the town might well have gone on to Kate Hamilton's for a few drinks and some supper. Located somewhere at the Leicester Square end of Panton Street, this was the most infamous night-house of the many in the Haymarket entertainment quarter. After ringing the bell at an unremarkable street door and successfully negotiating your way past two 'janitors' (i.e., bouncers), you went down a long passage into a large room with a small dance floor and tables and chairs strewn about. The place had no licence for music and dancing, or indeed for after-hours drinking, but that did not stop all these activities taking place. The night-house's centrepiece was its eponymous proprietor. Looking back to the 1860s, a rake of the day later painted this wonderful little word-picture of her: 'Kate Hamilton at this period must have weighed at least twenty stone, and had as ludicrous a physiognomy as any weather-beaten Deal pilot. Seated on a raised platform, with a bodice cut very low, this freak of nature sipped champagne steadily from midnight until daylight, and shook like a blancmange every time she laughed.' Despite presiding nightly over scenes which, whether moral or immoral, were certainly illegal, Kate was nevertheless said to be a well respected member of the congregation of a well known church and to be in the *Court Guide* as occupying a house in a good street.

Of course, anyone with eyes could see that under the glitter of Haymarket in the middle decades of the 19th century lay a terrible social evil. After witnessing what he called the 'lamentable Haymarket march past' between the hours of 11.00pm and 1.00am, Hippolyte Taine made the observation that 'the impression is not one of debauchery, but of abject, miserable poverty. One is sickened and wounded by this deplorable procession in those monumental streets. It seemed as if I were watching a march past of dead women.' In the 1870s, by which time the state of affairs after midnight in Haymarket and Panton Street had reached such a pitch that it could not be allowed to continue, English reformers came to share Taine's viewpoint. Local authorities and the purity lobby (consisting of prostitutes' rescue houses and the Vice Society, the site of whose headquarters you pass on the walk) joined forces to press for stricter police control of the streets and the suppression of prostitutes' favourite haunts.

By 1874 all the Haymarket night-houses had been closed; Kate Hamilton's was the last to go. As the crusading Superintendent Dunlop of the Metropolitan Police reported: 'Kate Hamilton was present when police entered with a warrant, and was crying bitterly saying that she supposed there was nothing for her now but the workhouse.' Four years later the Argyll Rooms followed suit. Having been deprived of its music and dancing licence, it closed its doors for the last time on 30 November 1878.

After the Haymarket clampdown during and after the 1870s, street prostitution remained a feature of the Strand, especially the Charing Cross end, into the 20th century. But it no longer coloured the character of the whole area as it had done before the Victorian repression movement got into its full stride.

THE STRAND AND HAYMARKET WALK

Start: Temple underground station (District and Circle lines). On sundays when Temple station is closed, use Blackfriars (also District and Circle lines), 550yd (500m) to the east.

Finish: Piccadilly Circus underground station (Piccadilly and Bakerloo lines).

Length: 2 miles (3.2km).

Refreshments: There are all kinds of places to eat and drink along this route.

Route note: Near the beginning of the walk there is a gated section (Clement's Inn). If this is closed, follow the alternative route shown by the dotted line on the map.

Come out of Temple station, turn left up the steps and cross Temple Place into Arundel Street. The modern office block on the left covers two former streets: Norfolk Street, running parallel to Arundel Street, and Howard Street, running at right-angles, connecting Arundel Street to

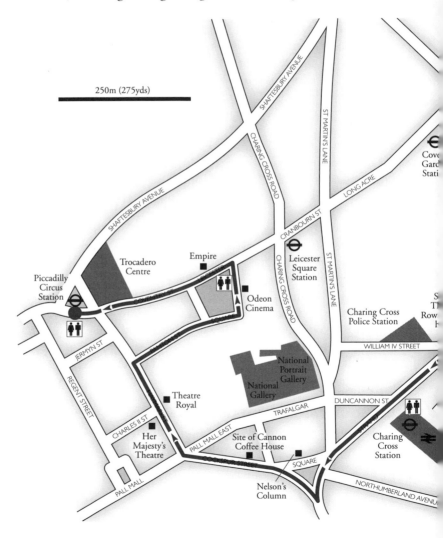

Surrey Street. The actor Will Mountfort lived in Howard Street. Returning home on 9 December 1692 he was waylaid by two young men – boys, really – Captain Richard Hill, aged just 15, and Lord Mohun, aged 16. The latter was just starting out on his notorious career as a rake and duellist. Hill was jealous of Mountfort's friendship with a certain actress with whom he fancied himself in love. While Mohun engaged the 33-year-old Mountfort in conversation, Hill approached from behind and stabbed him in the back. Mohun was tried for murder in the House of Lords but acquitted. Hill escaped overseas, serving as a volunteer soldier before returning in the early 18th century to claim – and receive – a pardon.

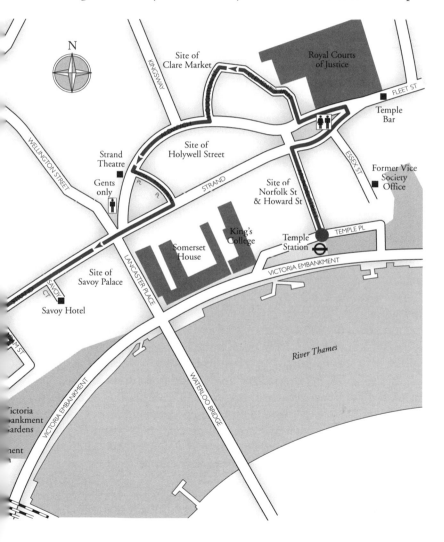

A century later the greatest Shakespeare forgery of all time was conceived and hatched at 55 Norfolk Street, home of the Ireland family. In 1794 19-year-old William Ireland, an apprentice property conveyancer, pretended he had gained access to a secret cache of Shakespeare documents and began producing items from it, apparently to please his Shakespeare-addicted father. To start with the forgeries were simple things like title deeds, but ultimately they came to include poems and even a whole play. Besides Ireland senior, many eminent people were taken in by the forgeries, and the play, *Vortigern and Rowena*, was even presented at the Drury Lane Theatre, with Richard Brinsley Sheridan as producer and the great John Philip Kemble playing the lead. However, it was laughed off stage before the end. When Ireland senior was accused of the forgeries, his son had to confess, leading to an estrangement between the two which had still not been healed when Ireland senior died in 1800. Ironically, young William, who lived on until 1835, turned out to be not a bad writer on his own account, and earned a living with his pen for the rest of his life.

At the top of Arundel Street turn right into the Strand. The modern office block on the right (No 190) stands on the site of, among other premises, a tobacconist's shop above which, in the mid-1950s, Soviet spy Peter Kroger rented a room for his antiquarian book business. He had a suitably international clientele. Books containing microdots were regularly mailed abroad to 'overseas customers'. And 'customers' and foreign 'booksellers' often visited the shop on UK 'buying trips'. Kroger's spy ring, based at his bungalow home in suburban Ruislip, was eventually broken up in 1961 and Kroger, his wife and three others were sentenced to long prison terms for passing on information about Britain's latest anti-submarine detection equipment. In 1969 the Krogers were freed to the Soviet Union in an exchange.

Continue along the Strand. Second on the right is Essex Street. No 31, near the far end on the left, was the office of the 19th century Society for the Suppression of Vice. Founded in 1802, the Vice Society was the Victorians' main weapon in the war against pornography and prostitution. Most of its battles were fought in the courts, but shortage of funds prevented it from bringing any more legal actions after 1880. By then it had in any case, in the words of one historian, freed London from its most determined pornographers and also from its reputation as the smut capital of Europe. One can't help wondering what the society did with its hoard of obscene material when it finally shut down. Apparently there was over five tons of the stuff in its vaults.

Continue along the Strand, round the curve (⚏ left on traffic island). Just beyond Twinings, the tea merchants, is 217 Strand, now the Law Courts branch of NatWest Bank. In the 1850s this was an old-established bank called Strahan, Paul and Bates. Hit by bad debts from collieries, the three partners desperately tried to keep the business afloat by selling several hundred thousand pounds worth of securities deposited with them for safekeeping. The fraud failed, and in 1855 the bank went under with liabilities of £750,000, millions in today's money. This was the first and most shocking of a series of huge bank frauds which helped make the City notorious as a financial jungle in the second half of the 19th century (see the City chapter). All three partners were sentenced to transportation for 14 years; not so long before, they would have been hanged (see the Fauntleroy case, page 117).

Looking ahead along the Strand you can see a pedestal in the middle of the road with a strange-looking beast on top. This marks the site of Temple Bar, one of the old gateways into the City of London. Like other City gates, particularly the one at the south end of London Bridge (see page 20), Temple Bar was used to display the heads and other body parts of executed traitors. The heads of the Rye House plotters, executed in 1683, were among the first to be spiked here. People could get a closer look at them by hiring a telescope for a halfpenny.

Now turn left across the pedestrian crossing to the Royal Courts of Justice and turn left again in front of them. City fraudster Whittaker Wright committed suicide in the courts in 1904 (see page 44). In the 18th century, over one hundred years before the courts were built, there was a tavern-cum-brothel here called the Star, roughly where the main entrance to the courts is today. On 1 July 1749 three sailors from HMS *Grafton* visited the brothel and had their watches and money stolen by the girls. When they complained they were thrown out by the bouncers. Having collected a gang of mates, they returned to the brothel and trashed it, burning all the furniture on a bonfire in the middle of the street. The incident sparked off one of London's regular bawdy-house riots – violent anti-brothel pogroms usually carried out by the capital's unruly apprentices. On this particular occasion soldiers had to be called out to restore order. The three sailors escaped arrest, but a drunken passer-by, who had been out celebrating his birthday, was unluckily caught up in the affray and arrested. Farce turned to tragedy when the poor boy, convicted on the no-doubt perjured evidence of the brothel-keeper, was executed at Tyburn on 28 October.

When you draw abreast of the far end of St Clement Danes Church, turn right through the gates into Clement's Inn (if they're closed, see Route Note at start of walk). Follow this round as it bends left and then right, and go up the steps at the end into Clement's Inn Passage. This brings you to the centre of the campus of the London School of Economics, built at the beginning of the 20th century on the site of Clare Market and surrounding streets, including Vere Street. A century earlier the market district was notorious as a meeting place for gay men. At the White Swan pub in Vere Street landlord James Cook operated a gay club and brothel known as the Vere Street Coterie. The club was raided in July 1810 and 27 people were arrested; six were tried and sent to prison, but only after they had first endured a brutal pillory session. (The walk passes the pillory site later.)

Turn left into Houghton Street and walk on down to the junction with Aldwych, a new road completed in 1905; before that, Houghton Street led into Maypole Alley. In the autumn of 1724, after his second and more dramatic escape from Newgate prison, Jack Sheppard, 18th century London's most notorious highwayman, got drunk with his mother at the Sheers Tavern in Maypole Alley. He was re-arrested in the tavern, taken back to Newgate and watched night and day until 16 November, when he was executed at Tyburn in front of a huge crowd.

The Aldwych development also obliterated Holywell Street, which lay just beyond Maypole Alley. In the 19th century Holywell Street was the centre of London's pornography trade. Of its ninety or so retailers of erotica, the most prolific and notorious was William Dugdale. An odious man, said to have been involved in the 1820 Cato Street plot to murder the Cabinet, Dugdale turned to porn in the late 1820s. Operating from 37 Holywell Street, he published such titles as *Betsy Thoughtless*, 'a most spicy and piquant narrative of a young girl obliged to excoriate her sweetheart's bum before he could ravish her maidenhead'. After at least ten prison sentences, Dugdale died in the Clerkenwell House of Correction in 1868. By then Holywell Street's glory days were long since over, terminated by the Obscene Publications Act of 1857.

Turn right on Aldwych and cross Kingsway. On 18 February 1996 Aldwych hit the headlines when a bus blew up here, killing five people. It turned out later that one of the dead, Edward O'Brien, was a member of the IRA. He was probably on his way to the City or Docklands to plant a bomb when it exploded prematurely.

Cross Drury Lane and carry on past the Meridien Hotel. Just beyond it, look out for the Ivor Novello blue plaque at the entrance to Waldorf Chambers. Britain's most famous matinee idol and songwriter, Novello was caught up in a scandal in World War II when he fraudulently obtained extra petrol rations to allow him to drive to his country home at weekends from his luxury flat here. He was sentenced to a month in Wormwood Scrubs prison. The whole experience understandably shattered him, and is said to have contributed to his death seven years later in 1951.

Just beyond Novello's former home is the Strand Theatre. One night in April 1870 police arrested two young men as they were leaving the theatre. Both were dressed in women's clothing. It turned out that the men in question *Ernest Boulton and Frederick Park* – the men in question – formed a ménage à trois with Lord Arthur Clinton, duke's son and MP. The resulting buggery trial (not involving Clinton, who died of scarlet fever before the case came to court) was the greatest homosexual scandal of the mid-Victorian period. Boulton and Park were acquitted, but that did not stop this limerick doing the rounds of the West End clubs:

> There was an old person of Sark
> Who buggered a pig in the dark;
> The swine in surprise
> Murmured, God blast your eyes,
> Do you take me for Boulton or Park?

Turn left across Aldwych (it's one-way, so take care to look right on both sides of the road) and go down the steps into India Place, followed by Montreal Place. This brings you back onto the Strand opposite (slightly to the left) King's College, part of London University. In 1831 two notorious bodysnatchers, John Bishop and Thomas Williams, tried to sell a corpse to Richard Partridge, an anatomy instructor in the college's medical school. By chance Partridge recognized the body as that of an Italian boy who had made a living exhibiting white mice in the streets – the college entrance had been one of his favourite pitches. Pretending he needed change for a £50 note, Partridge left the room and called the police. The men were arrested, and confessed to murdering the boy by drowning him in a well in Bethnal Green. Bishop also confessed to two other 'burking' murders and the sale of 500–1000 bodies. Both men were hanged outside Newgate prison on 5 December 1831 in front of a crowd estimated at 30,000. Three people were killed when the crowd stampeded (see page 30).

Notoriety attached itself to King's College again in 1946 when Special Branch officers turned up and arrested nuclear-physics lecturer Dr Alan Nunn May, who for some years had been passing information and microscopic samples of uranium to the Soviets via a Russian agent in Canada. Sentenced to 10 years in prison, May was released in 1952 and emigrated to Ghana, where he worked as a physics professor.

Cross the Strand at the lights and turn right in front of Somerset House. Walk as far as Lancaster Place (♨ – men only – to right in Wellington Place), which leads to Waterloo Bridge. It was at the bus-stop at the far end of the bridge (left-hand side) that Bulgarian writer and emigré critic Georgi Markov was fatally wounded by an assassin on the evening of 7 September 1978. The murderer, presumably acting on the orders of the Bulgarian secret police, who wanted to stop Markov's anti-government broadcasts on the BBC, Radio Free Europe and other stations, used a specially adapted umbrella to implant a tiny ball containing deadly poison in Markov's leg. Markov died in hospital four days later.

Cross Lancaster Place and continue along the Strand. First on the left, Savoy Street covers part of Savoy Palace, cleared to make way for the building of Waterloo Bridge in the early 19th century. In April 1772, when the old palace was an army barracks, Isaac Bickerstaffe, the leading playwright of the day, propositioned a guardsman at the barracks. Instead of responding to his advances – as, until well into the 20th century, many London soldiers traditionally did in order to supplement their meagre pay (see page 130) – the soldier stole his seal, watch and ring and tried to blackmail him. The scandal got into the papers and Bickerstaffe was forced to flee abroad.

Continue along the Strand. Look out on the left for the arched entrance to Savoy Buildings, opposite the Strand Palace Hotel. The plaque records the existence nearby of a once-notorious tavern called the Coal Hole, and mentions the fact that the dissolute actor Edmund Kean used to frequent it. It does not mention 'Chief Baron' Nicholson and his infamous Judge and Jury Club, of which more in a minute.

Next on the left (opposite Exeter Street) is Savoy Court, leading to the Savoy Hotel. Hotel and Court were built on the site of Beaufort Buildings, where William Byrd, who appears in the Covent Garden chapter, lodged from 1717 to 1719. A widower in his early 40s with a powerful sex drive, Byrd took full advantage of the facilities on offer in and around Covent Garden to satisfy his desires. But the maid at Beaufort Buildings was also obliging: in early 1718, at least, he regularly kissed her until his 'seed ran'. Two centuries after Byrd's time the Savoy Hotel was the scene of a killing, when Marguerite Fahmy shot her Egyptian playboy husband in Suite 41 on the fourth floor in 1923. Although only 22, Ali Kamel Fahmy Bey had already proved himself a sexual pervert with violent tendencies. Yet Marguerite's defence lawyer cunningly chose not to play that card at her trial. Instead he convinced the jury that she had pulled the trigger by mistake, so getting her off not only a charge of murder but also one of manslaughter.

Carry on along the Strand. Next on the left is Carting Lane. On the corner here is the modern-day Coal Hole pub. Wherever the original Coal Hole was – and it is difficult to be more precise other than that it was within the historic precincts of the Savoy – it was certainly the scene of Nicholson's Judge and Jury Club, the most notorious of several similar clubs operating in London in the mid-19th century. Exploiting the verbatim reports in the downmarket press of all the most sensational divorce cases of the day, judge and jury clubs staged mock versions of these real-life trials, highlighting, for the amusement of the paying audience, the naughtiest and the funniest bits.

At the Coal Hole, Renton Nicholson played the judge (hence his nickname of Chief Baron), actors and hack writers the barristers and witnesses, and the audience the jury. The show closed with a 'pose plastique', the depiction of some well known painting or sculpture by unmoving girls dressed in flesh-coloured tights so as to look naked. By modern standards Nicholson's club was embarrassingly tame, but in its day it was scandalous.

Continue along the Strand. Next on the left is the arched entrance to Shell-Mex House. In 1950 this was still the wartime office of the Atomic Energy Division of the Ministry of Supply. In February that year a meeting was set up to which 36-year-old German-born Klaus Fuchs, a senior official at the Harwell Atomic Energy Establishment, was invited. However, it was literally a set-up for the purpose of the meeting, duly carried out, was Fuchs's arrest and the termination of his eight-year double life as a Soviet spy. During that time he had passed on secret information which it is estimated saved the Soviets two years in their development of the atom bomb. Fuchs spent nine years in prison before being deported to East Germany, where he died in 1988.

Beyond Shell-Mex House, take the first left into Adam Street and then the first right into John Adam Street. Further along on the right, on the corner of Durham House Street, you come to No 16, which, as the blue plaque indicates, covers the site of a house once lived in by artist Thomas Rowlandson. Rowlandson is well known for his earthy, sometimes bawdy drawings and watercolours depicting English scenes and people in the late 18th and early 19th centuries. What he is not so well known for – for obvious reasons – is his considerable output of erotica. Holywell Street was no doubt a major market for this side of his work.

On the far side of Durham House, turn right into George Court and climb the steps back up to the Strand. Directly opposite, set back from the road, with a red phone box outside and posters on the railings, is Charing Cross Police Station. Here, wrapped in plastic bags and stored on shelves in large vaults, is all the obscene material seized from clubs and porn shops in Soho, London's current red-light district (see Chapter 7). Turn left and walk on to the forecourt of Charing Cross station (⚎ in station). In 1927 the station played a role in a murder known to history as the Charing Cross Trunk Murder. After the dismembered body of a woman was found in a trunk in the left-luggage office, a masterpiece of detection led police to 35-year-old estate agent John Robinson. He had met the victim – Minnie Bonati – at Victoria and taken her to his office nearby for sex. After a row, presumably over money, he had suffocated her while trying, so he said, to stifle her shouts. His claim of accidental death might have saved him had he not disposed of her body in such a brutal manner.

Carry on past the station until you come to Northumberland Street, on the left. Before the Embankment was built, this led directly to the riverside. At the river end, on the left-hand side, magistrate Sir Edmund Berry Godfrey had a house and timber yard in the 1670s. On 12 October 1678 he set out from his house to an address near St Clement Danes Church. He never got there. Five days later his body was found in a ditch at the bottom of Primrose Hill. He had been strangled and then run through with his own sword. Three men were executed for his murder on the strength of a fourth man's confession, but that man subsequently retracted his statement and admitted perjuring himself. Since then Godfrey's death has become a classic historical whodunnit. The most likely explanation is that it was something to do with the fictitious Popish Plot, an alleged Catholic conspiracy to murder Charles II and replace him with his more aggressively Catholic brother, the Duke of York (later James II).

Nearer this end of Northumberland Street, at No 2 (left-hand side), the *Pall Mall Gazette* used to have its offices. In 1885 its campaigning editor, William Stead, published a courageous series of articles exposing the related scandals of child prostitution and the white slave trade. Unfortunately Stead had 'bought' a young girl himself in order to get evidence, and so exposed himself to prosecution. He duly went to prison for three months and was sacked from his job. But the sensation caused by the notorious 'Maiden Tribute to Babylon' articles led to immediate changes in the law, making it much harder for the brothels responsible for child prostitution to operate.

Continue to the end of the Strand. Cross Northumberland Avenue and carry on to the traffic island in the middle of Whitehall. The equestrian statue of Charles I, placed here in 1675, marks the approximate site of the historic, pre-Trafalgar Square road junction called Charing Cross. Here on 17 October 1660, within sight of the Banqueting House of Whitehall Palace where Charles I had been beheaded in 1649, eight of the men who had signed the king's death warrant were themselves executed, suffering the traditional fate of traitors – hanging, drawing and quartering. Diarist John Evelyn 'met their quarters, mangled and cut and reeking as they were brought from the gallows in baskets on a hurdle'. Three days later Samuel Pepys saw some of the body parts displayed on spikes on one of the City gates.

Behind the statue of Charles I is Nelson's Column. In the 1920s the notorious Scottish conman Arthur Fergusson, posing as a civil servant, succeeded in selling the column to a gullible American tourist for £6000. During the course of his brief but lucrative career, Fergusson also 'sold' Buckingham Palace, Big Ben, the White House and the Statue of Liberty. A pity he didn't put his talents to more legitimate use: he could have made a fortune.

Now cross to the other side of Whitehall and turn right across The Mall. Bearing left round the corner, continue on into Cockspur Street. Canada House, on the right, stands on the site of the Cannon Coffee House at No 1 Cockspur Street. In 1763 Casanova came here with his friend, MP's son and future Customs Commissioner Wellbore Agar, and two prostitutes, one English and one French. Casanova, deeply depressed at the time thanks to a failed conquest, was hardly an enthusiastic participant in the adventure. Agar sought to cheer him up by getting the English girl to dance the hornpipe naked. The usual blind musicians were wheeled in and the English girl did her dance, with Agar and the French girl – both naked too – joining in. Agar, by now in high spirits, then copulated with the two girls. The world's most notorious seducer, meanwhile, could hardly raise a smile, let alone anything else.

Carry on to the end of Cockspur Street (where it meets Pall Mall) and cross right at the lights into Haymarket, walking up the right-hand side of the street. On the left is Her Majesty's Theatre, originally London's opera house and the starting point for the awful Haymarket promenade witnessed by Taine, Dostoevsky and others in the 1850s and 1860s. Walk through the portico of the Theatre Royal, built in 1820.

The original Haymarket Theatre, dating from about a century earlier, was just north of it, roughly where King's House is now at No 10. In the 18th century it was part-owned by the 2nd Duke of Montagu, a notorious practical joker. Once he decided to prove his notion that people would believe anything, especially if they read it in the papers. So he put out an ad saying that on 16 January 1749 a magician would perform certain amazing feats at the Haymarket Theatre, including squeezing into a quart bottle and singing a song therein. On the night in question the house was, as the duke predicted, packed. However, when no performer appeared, the audience, realizing it had been duped, trashed the theatre and burnt all the contents in the street, like the sailors at the Star. Several people were killed during the riot. The duke had made his point, but at a high price.

Continue up Haymarket – crossing Orange Street – as far as Panton Street. In 1761 Swiss miniature painter Théodore Gardelle, drinking companion of William Hogarth, was hanged at this street junction for the murder of his Leicester Square landlady. Young William Hickey, encountered in Chapter 5, witnessed the execution. Afterwards Gardelle's corpse was hung in chains on Hounslow Heath, west of London. Two years later, by which time the skeleton had been picked clean, Hickey rode underneath it and knocked a couple of its toes off! Half a century later the members of the gay club known as the Vere Street Coterie (see page 98) stood for an hour in the pillory here before beginning their prison sentences. According to a report in the *Morning Herald*, 'upwards of fifty women were permitted to stand in a ring and assail them with mud, dead cats, rotten eggs, potatoes and buckets of grub, offal and dung, which were brought by a number of butchers' men from St James's Market'. The prisoners were lucky to get back to the relative safety of gaol alive.

Turn right into Panton Street, in the 1860s a sink of iniquity. Cross Oxendon Street and Whitcomb Street. Kate Hamilton's notorious night-house was somewhere here, probably on the left-hand side, though without a precise address it is impossible to be sure.

Continue along the south side of Leicester Square. Just beyond St Martin's Street, the Hampshire Hotel stands on the site of 36 Leicester Square, where the Swiss painter Gardelle murdered his landlady, Mrs Anna King, allegedly because she had spurned his advances. Having dismembered her body and tried to burn it, he stuffed her entrails 'into the boghouse' where they were discovered by the cleaner, who raised the alarm. Were it not for the fact that Leicester House, at the top of the square, was then occupied by members of the royal family, Gardelle would have been hanged outside the scene of his crime.

Turn left up the east side of the square. The Odeon cinema stands on the site of 27 Leicester Square, an 18th century bagnio associated with the notorious Mary Tofts rabbit hoax. Mary Tofts came from Godalming, where she claimed to have been so frightened by rabbits in a field that she started giving birth to rabbits herself. Somehow she convinced royal surgeon Nathaniel St André, who brought her to London in December 1726, lodging her in Lacy's bagnio. Just four days later Mary was caught buying rabbits and the whole absurd fraud – which was presumably perpetrated for financial gain and which caused a sensation in London – was exposed. Having confessed, Mary returned to Godalming. St André, not surprisingly, was disgraced.

Looking into the centre of the square, spare a thought for notorious swindler Baron Albert Grant (see page 43). At the height of his fame, when he had ambitions to be a public benefactor, Grant bought Leicester Square, then a glorified rubbish dump, did it up, planted a statue of Shakespeare in the middle and presented the square to the public on 2 July 1874. But his reputation in the City, if not in the country, was already suspect, and on the day of the presentation ceremony some joker paid sandwich men to walk round the square with lists of Grant's defaulting companies on one side of their boards and this witty couplet (referring to Grant's worthless Italian title) on the other:

> Honours a king can give, honour he can't;
> And Grant without honour is a Baron Grant.

Carry on up the square to the northeast corner (⛎) and turn left to reach the Empire cinema, on your right. In the 1890s the Empire was a variety theatre. The Haymarket and surrounding streets may have been cleaned up by that time, but the variety theatres and music halls remained notorious prostitutes' hunting grounds. The Empire, with its long bars and wide promenades behind the auditorium, was the most notorious of the lot. In 1894 Mrs Ormiston Chant, the Mary Whitehouse of the day, succeeded in persuading the London County Council that the Empire should have its music and dance licence renewed only if it erected screens between the auditorium and the promenades, partly to protect the audience from the prostitutes and partly to prevent men lounging among the prostitutes at the bar having their blood roused by the sight of the scantily dressed dancing girls on stage. On the first night the new screens appeared (3 November 1894), the audience tore them down, a youthful Winston Churchill assisting in the demolition work. The following year the Empire – whose takings had plummeted as a result of the screens – got them removed officially, and the girls and the top-hatted swells returned to the theatre – at least until after World War I, when the Empire went out of fashion.

Walk straight on out of the square along the right-hand side of New Coventry Street and continue into Coventry Street. When you get to Great Windmill Street you are standing next to the Trocadero Centre, which itself stands on the site of the notorious Argyll Rooms, one of the main institutions of the Haymarket Sodom and Gomorrah in the mid-19th century. Now continue along Coventry Street to Piccadilly underground station (⛎), where the walk ends.

Soho
Porn Trade and Gang Warfare

North of Leicester Square and south of Oxford Street lies the cosmopolitan quarter of Soho, home to successive waves of European immigrants from the 17th century French Huguenots onwards. In the 19th century, when the Strand and Haymarket together hosted London's main female flesh market, Soho was one of the seedy backwaters to which the prostitutes took their clients. After World War I, as social and economic changes led to the tide of prostitution flowing north and west to Piccadilly and Mayfair, Soho emerged as the main centre of London's sex trade. Since then it has been the most notorious red-light district not only in London but throughout the country. And in the late 1940s and 1950s it enjoyed further notoriety as the stage on which London's two main gangland bosses played out their battle for control of the capital's underworld.

The Square Mile of Vice
In Soho, as in earlier red-light districts, girls were on the streets mainly from the late afternoon onwards, as shops and offices closed. In Glasshouse Street a shift of heavily made-up older professionals plied their trade from midnight until dawn. Between the wars many of Soho's prostitutes were professional Frenchwomen, known locally as Fifis. You could tell them immediately by their immaculate clothes and houses, and often by their gold ankle-chains. By the 1950s there were reckoned to be some 5000 prostitutes on London's streets. All were north of Piccadilly and Coventry Street, almost exactly the reverse of the situation a century before. Mayfair and Piccadilly Circus had their fair share, but Soho was full of them. One night in the 1950s a policeman walking along Shaftesbury Avenue up to Cambridge Circus counted no fewer than 100 girls soliciting.

Although Soho's prostitutes were part of the local community and accepted by other residents, public opinion generally was increasingly in favour of sweeping them off the streets. This was finally achieved in 1959 by the historic Street Offences Act. Until that time the normal punishment for soliciting was a 40s fine, and that fine was the same no matter how many convictions you had. Since 40s itself was no deterrent, many girls had hundreds of convictions to their name. The 1959 Act worked by providing imprisonment as the punishment for the third offence. Overnight, the West End's streets were cleared of prostitutes. Police said it was as though they had been vacuumed up. In the first quarter after the act came into force, prosecutions for soliciting were down by an amazing 90%.

Many of Soho's prostitutes worked for ponces. Traditionally these were foreign, because the average British-born criminal disdained to soil his hands with such a sleazy trade. One of the most notorious ponces in 1920s Soho was Jamaican Eddie Manning, reviled as the wickedest man in London – no doubt partly because he was black. Having come to England in 1916 to work in a munitions factory, he turned to pimping and by 1919 was running up to a dozen girls from his flat in Lisle Street and a basement café in Berwick Street that he managed with his Greek girlfriend. Manning's unsavoury career – which embraced drugs as well as sex – came to an end when he was gaoled in 1929. He died two years later.

Among his fellow Soho operators in the 1920s were Casimir Micheletti, a Frenchman, and Juan Antonio Castanar, a Spaniard. Castanar's dancing school in Archer Street (where, incidentally, the tango was first danced in England) doubled as a useful recruiting agency for the white slave trade. This involved European girls who went to work as upmarket prostitutes in exotic foreign locations such as South America and China. Micheletti and Castanar were bitter rivals, and remained so even after both were deported in 1929. The following year the Spaniard shot the Frenchman dead.

Far and away the most notorious vice gang in 1930s and 1940s London was the Messina family. The five Messina brothers – Alfredo, Attilio, Carmelo, Eugene and Salvatore – were the children of a Maltese mother and a Sicilian father. Having been thrown out of Alexandria, where they had been brought up in the brothel trade, the brothers moved to London in the mid-1930s. Here they rapidly built up a lucrative vice ring, importing girls from the Continent, marrying them to impoverished Englishmen so that they could not be deported, and installing them in luxury flats. These were mainly in Mayfair (see page 129) and Knightsbridge, but they ran girls in Soho too. Hermione Hindin and Georgette Borg, for example, who shared the suburban home of Alfredo, arguably the worst of the Messinas, worked out of 7 Kingly Street, Soho.

By a mixture of threats and actual violence the brothers enforced a harsh discipline in their little sex army. Many of their foreign girls, lured across the Channel with promises of the good life, were kept in England against their will. When working they were permitted to spend no longer than ten minutes with clients, not even enough to take their clothes off. By 1947 the Messinas, driving around in Rolls Royces and openly collecting money from their girls, had become so arrogant and powerful that the Home Secretary was forced to admit in Parliament that nothing could be done to stop them: the problem was that no one was prepared to risk testifying against them.

Eventually campaigning crime reporter Duncan Webb undertook to expose the Messinas for his paper, the *Sunday People*. Following a series of thoroughly researched articles in September and October 1950, three of the brothers fled to the Continent and the other two were gaoled. However, their empire – not, as often claimed, the dominant one in the West End, simply the best-organized and most widely known – survived. Retired prostitutes carried on collecting money in London and sending it over to the Continent. Messina brothers overseas continued to send fresh recruits to London. As late as 1970, apparently, certain police officers were aware that the Messinas still owned at least half a dozen brothels in Mayfair.

One of the last foreign ponces in the Soho sex trade was Belgian Johnny, real name Jean Hubert. Having come to London in 1940 with the Free Belgian forces, Hubert's earnings from two women plus his French-born wife, Germaine Borelli, who worked out of a flat in Wardour Street, enabled him to drive around in a Jaguar, revelling in his reputation as a 'flash ponce'. But his good fortune did not last: he was deported in 1960.

By this time the Soho vice trade was dominated by the Syndicate, an organization led by Bernie Silver and Big Frank Mifsud. Born in Stoke Newington, Silver served in the Parachute Regiment before entering the sex trade as a Messina henchman. His partner, Mifsud, was an ex-traffic policeman from Malta (many Maltese were involved in Soho vice). Based at B. Silver and W. Cooper, estate agents of 34 Romilly Street, the Syndicate both rented small flats at exorbitant rents to prostitutes and operated its own string of girls. Silver was prosecuted for living on immoral earnings in 1956, but acquitted. The Syndicate also owned about twenty strip clubs (the first ones opened in Soho in 1954), and ran gambling joints and drinking dives, mostly illegal. Police claimed, somewhat incredibly, that at its peak – and it survived for fifteen years – the Syndicate was making £100,000 a week. Other important figures in Soho's sex trade in the 1950s and 1960s were John Mason and Jimmy Humphreys. Humphreys, a south Londoner from the Old Kent Road, married Rusty Gaynor, queen of the Soho strippers, in 1964. Together they ran at least three clubs in Soho, making enough to buy a flat in Dean Street and a 14-bedroomed manor house in Kent. Humphreys' business diaries later played a key role in police corruption trials in the 1970s.

In the permissive era of the 1960s, Soho's vice barons expanded their empires. After the 1959 Street Offences Act, prostitutes needed new ways of meeting their clients, so the vice barons obligingly opened all kinds of new places with just that purpose in mind – hostess bars, strip clubs, saunas, bogus massage parlours and the like. These new establishments did not have alcohol licences, so mock champagne, non-alcoholic wine and 'near-beer' were provided instead, of course at hugely inflated prices.

Vice bosses also moved into porn shops. Soho had always had its handful of discreet porn shops selling erotica and poorly produced obscene books. But from the mid-1960s onwards the square mile of vice witnessed a boom in hard-core pornography, fuelled by imports from Sweden and Denmark, where the censorship laws had recently been relaxed. By 1970 Soho had at least forty porn shops, some of them quite large and with prominent window displays that left little to the imagination. Public opposition to these shops was vocal, but there was little the authorities could do. One problem was that the owners of the shops – Silver, Mifsud and the other leading Soho pornographers – operated behind frontmen who were paid to take the rap in the event of a police raid. Another and far bigger problem was that Soho's immensely wealthy pornographers had succeeded in corrupting the very police who should have been trying to put them out of business. Senior Scotland Yard officers on the payroll included Chief Superintendent Bill Moody, the head of the Obscene Publications Squad, Commander Wallace Virgo, head of the CID, and Commander Kenneth Drury, head of the Flying Squad.

The sums involved in paying off the police were quite enormous: up to £14,000 just to open a porn shop, and thereafter £500 a week to keep it open. Then there were the dinners out, the jewellery for the wives, and the foreign holidays. In return, the pornographers were permitted to bring out hard-core porn from the back room or under the counter, where it was normally kept, and display it in the main part of the shop, which was of course illegal. They were also given advance warning of raids so that any illicit material on display could be safely hidden away. John Mason was even allowed to buy seized pornography awaiting destruction from the Obscene Publications Squad's store in the basement of Holborn police station (the store is now underneath Charing Cross police station – see page 101).

No effective action was taken to root out police corruption until the *Sunday People* published a series of articles in November 1971 and February 1972. These not only named the hitherto faceless porn barons in Soho but also demonstrated links between them and the police. Most damaging was a photograph of Ken Drury, head of the Flying Squad, on holiday in Cyprus with Jimmy Humphreys. A four-year secret investigation followed, at the end of which 15 Metropolitan Police officers were arrested; of these, 13 were subsequently sent to prison, including Moody and Virgo, who each got 12 years (Virgo was released less than a year later on medical grounds). The corruption trials in the mid-1970s were the biggest police scandal since 1877, when fully one-third of Scotland Yard's detectives were jailed for taking bribes (see page 147).

Meanwhile, in 1974, the *News of the World* had exposed Silver and his prostitution rackets. He was gaoled for six years for living on immoral earnings, the same charge on which he had been acquitted 18 years earlier. Silver's partner Mifsud retired to Malta. John Mason got away to the Channel Islands. Jimmy Humphreys was gaoled for eight years for attacking one of his wife's former lovers, but pardoned after serving fewer than three as a reward for helping nail Drury, Moody, Virgo and the other bent coppers. A note of tragedy was sounded when Silver's prostitute wife, Albertine Falzon, killed herself by jumping from the window of her business flat in Peter Street.

Many Soho residents hoped that the crackdown on leading pornographers and corrupt policemen in the mid-1970s would lead to a general clean-up of Soho's increasingly sleazy streets. But the police and Westminster City Council both failed to act. In fact, the Council tacitly encouraged the spread of the sex industry by allowing Soho's old houses and craft workshops to be converted into video booths, topless bars and other sex outlets. In 1977 the Soho sex trade occupied as many as 185 premises. It was only after the newly formed Soho Society persuaded Westminster Council to tighten up its licensing system in the early 1980s that this number was reduced to a more acceptable 35 by 1989. Soho's visible sex trade is now concentrated in the Brewer Street, Rupert Street and Walker's Court area, as you will see on the walk.

Gangland Soho

After World War II London's underworld was dominated by two men – Jack Spot and Billy Hill. The son of Polish Jews, Jack Spot (real name Comer; his nickname came from the fact that he was often in a spot of bother) hailed from Whitechapel. During the 1930s he put his street-fighting skills to good use by protecting Jewish businesses from anti-Semitic attacks. He is also said – or rather he claimed – to have played a prominent part in the Battle of Cable Street (see page 72). Billy Hill, by contrast, grew up in the old thieves' kitchen of Seven Dials (see page 88), where both his parents were well acquainted with the law. During the 1930s and 1940s he spent some fifteen years in gaol. He was particularly good with the 'chiv', or razor, gangland's standard weapon, and boasted of inventing the downwards slash so as to avoid cutting an artery, very important at a time of capital punishment.

During World War II Hill made a fortune stealing and selling black-market goods. When peace returned he was in a strong position to dominate London's underworld, but a badly timed spell in prison allowed Spot to come down from Leeds, where he had made his mark during the war, and establish himself in the capital.

Both men were drawn to Soho because of its many illegal gambling joints and drinking dens and its generally raffish atmosphere. Good old traditional British hard men, neither was interested in vice: that was for foreigners. As Spot said, 'We won't stand for ponces.' Spot in particular was a familiar cigar-smoking figure in Soho. The Modernaires Club in Old Compton Street was virtually his office.

Until the early 1950s, Spot and Hill were more colleagues than rivals, and the police more or less left them alone to keep the peace in the underworld. But by 1952 Hill, the better businessman of the two, began to outstrip Spot. Spot's bullion raid on Heathrow Airport failed, whereas Hill's 1952 hijack of a Post Office mail van in Eastcastle Street (more details on page 117) and his 1954 bullion heist in Holborn were spectacular successes. Many of Spot's henchmen started to go over to Hill, who was by now both wealthy and a celebrity both in and beyond the underworld.

In 1955 Hill brought his battle with Spot to a head by publicly accusing Spot of informing during the police investigation of an assault case way back in 1937. Spot sought revenge by planning an attack on Albert Dimes. Dimes, an Italian gangster and bookie based in Soho, was both one of Spot's biggest rivals in the racetrack-betting rackets business and also Hill's bodyguard; dealing with him would therefore kill two birds with one stone. On 11 August 1955 Spot attacked Dimes in Frith Street (more details on page 114). Dimes was badly injured, but so was Spot, which was one reason why gangland generally regarded the attack as a fatal mistake.

The Spot–Hill battle continued in the media, with Hill publishing a Duncan Webb-ghosted autobiography in which he claimed to be the undisputed king of Soho, and Spot telling his story in articles in the *Daily Sketch*. Hill won this contest, too. His book launch at Gennaro's Club in Dean Street was attended by a host of criminal and more respectable celebrities. Spot's *Daily Sketch* articles, meanwhile, were accompanied by an outspoken – and, for Spot, embarrassing – leader claiming that the 'ugly vice of crime' was 'tightening on Soho' and that it was time for the authorities to 'clean this cess-pool!'.

The following year the war ended in victory for Hill when Mad Frankie Fraser and other Hill henchmen slashed Spot on the steps of his Bayswater apartment block. Mad Frankie got seven years for this attack, but Hill had made it clear that he was now firmly in charge. In the underworld the joke went that 'Billy Hill's the boss – Jack Spot was very cut up about it'. Shortly after, Spot was evicted from his flat and declared bankrupt. Hill retired to a villa in sunny Spain, leaving the field to his protegés, the Krays (see The East End chapter).

THE SOHO WALK

Start and finish: Tottenham Court Road underground station (Northern and Central lines).

Length: 1¾ miles (2.8km).

Refreshments: There's no shortage of places in Soho, which is celebrated for its restaurants. At the halfway stage the walk passes Kettner's and the famous Coach and Horses pub in Romilly Street. Then comes Gerrard Street, the heart of Chinatown, with its many Chinese restaurants. Charlotte Street, near the end of the walk – not actually in Soho but culturally part of it – is also well known for its bars and restaurants.

Leave Tottenham Court Road underground station by the exit marked 'No 1 Exit, Oxford Street South Side', and turn right on Oxford Street. At the lights turn right into Charing Cross Road (♿ left in subway), passing on the right the Harmony sex shop, billed as Europe's largest licensed sex centre. Carry on for a little way and then turn right, by the Astoria, into Sutton Row. On the corner opposite the Astoria the Ann Summers shop is probably the best-known brand in the multi-million-pound sex empire created by brothers Ralph and David Gold. Besides Birmingham City Football Club, the Golds own downmarket papers like the *Daily Sport* and *Sunday Sport* and men's magazines such as *Playbirds* and *Park Lane*. The brothers got into the sex business after their mother Rose began selling 'pin-up' magazines from the shop in the front room of her East End house.

At the end of Sutton Row you come to Soho Square. At No 21, the corner house on the right, there was in the late 18th century a notorious upper-class brothel known as the White House, or Hooper's Hotel, after its proprietor, Thomas Hooper. Flagellation is said to have been a speciality of the house, and the Prince of Wales, later George IV, is claimed to have been a customer. On the other side of Sutton Row, St Patrick's Catholic Church stands on the site of 18th century Carlisle House, where Italian adventuress Theresa Cornelys hosted her lavish subscription masquerades in the 1760s. Popular with the upper classes, these were ideal for flirtations and sometimes more compromising encounters. Mrs Cornelys went bankrupt in 1772 and died a debtor in the Fleet prison (see page 34) a quarter of a century later.

Turn left by the church and then leave the square from the south side via Greek Street. When you get to the junction with Bateman Street you can see the sign for Greek Street's L'Escargot restaurant, ahead on the right. Just beyond L'Escargot is No 47, where master of seduction Giacomo Casanova lodged in 1764. Mrs Cornelys had been a conquest of his before she came

112

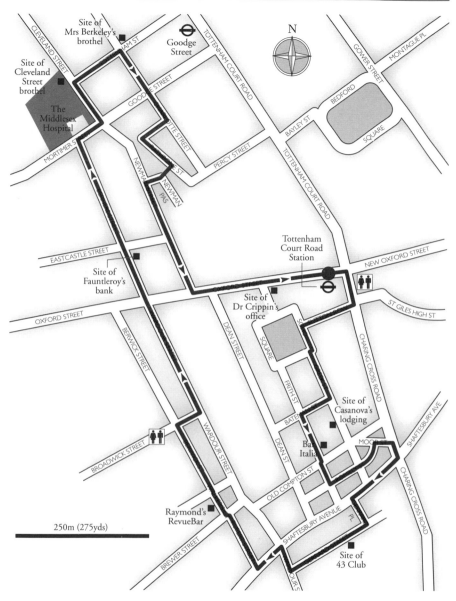

to England, and they had had a daughter, who lived with her mother. Mrs Cornelys's son by her husband, meanwhile, lived with Casanova on the Continent. In 1763 Mrs Cornelys asked Casanova to bring her son to England, hence his visit. He stayed eight months but was in Greek Street for only a short while before his hurried departure – penniless – on 11 March. If he had stayed he would probably have been hanged for forgery.

Turn right, into Bateman Street, and first left into Frith Street. Walk on down until you get to the Bar Italia on the left at 22 Frith Street (it has a large clock on the front). The so-called Battle of Frith Street started here on 11 August 1955 when gangster Jack Spot assaulted bookie Albert Dimes as a revenge attack on Billy Hill, Dimes's boss and Spot's rival for control of the London underworld. Wounded and bleeding, Dimes staggered towards Old Compton Street, taking refuge in the Continental Fruit Stores on the corner (now La Crêperie). The fight continued inside, with the proprietor's 13-stone wife belabouring the antagonists with a steel scoop. After a spell in hospital both men recovered, but the encounter is said to have contributed to Dimes's early death, aged 57, in 1972.

Looking to the right around the corner into Old Compton Street, you can see the Play 2 Win amusement arcade. On 4 September 1974, when it was called the Golden Goose, contract killer George Piggot, former henchman of notorious Notting Hill slum landlord Peter Rachman, who had died in 1962, walked in and shot dead Alfredo 'Italian Toni' Zomparelli. Zomparelli had just completed a prison sentence for killing 23-year-old David Knight at the Latin Quarter Club in Wardour Street (passed later in the walk) four years earlier, so, when Piggot confessed to Zomparelli's murder in 1979, Knight's elder brother Ronald, Soho club-owner and husband of the famous *Carry On* star Barbara Windsor, was tried for putting him up to it. He was acquitted in 1980. Piggot never revealed the true identity of his client, so who ordered the murder and why remain unknown.

Cross Old Compton Street and continue along Frith Street, turning first left into Romilly Street. Cross Greek Street. Just beyond the Coach and Horses pub on the left is the original 34 Romilly Street. Here the so-called Godfather of Soho, Bernie Silver, and his partner, Big Frank Mifsud ran their vice empire in the 1950s and 1960s. Today the seedy-looking building is still part of the sex trade, as a quick glance at the names on the two doorbells indicates – Monique and Brigitte, French models.

Carry on along Romilly Street to Cambridge Circus and turn right in front of the Palace Theatre into Shaftesbury Avenue. Shaftesbury Avenue was cut through the heart of Soho in the 1880s, obliterating King Street in the process. On 10 May 1853 the Chancellor of the Exchequer, William Gladstone, got into a spot of bother here, having 'rescued' a prostitute in Long Acre and brought her back to her King Street lodgings. (The precise nature and purpose of Gladstone's nocturnal social work among London's prostitutes is still a contentious subject.) As they approached the girl's house a young man stepped out of the shadows and threatened to reveal that the Chancellor had picked up a prostitute – unless Gladstone either gave him some money or got him a job in the Inland Revenue. Gladstone refused and the case came to court. The would-be blackmailer was sentenced to a year's hard labour, but Gladstone generously arranged for his release six months early.

From Shaftesbury Avenue, turn left into Gerrard Place and then right into Gerrard Street. In the hedonistic days of the 1920s the Loon Fung supermarket, on the left at 43 Gerrard Street, was the 43 Club, flagship of the notorious Kate Meyrick's night-club empire. When Mrs Meyrick's marriage to a Dublin doctor failed she brought her eight children to London and plunged into the burgeoning night-club business to earn a living. Although brilliantly successful and popular with the Bright Young Things, who enjoyed mixing with Soho's dangerous low life in her clubs, she frequently clashed with the police, and went to prison several times, usually for after-hours drinking but latterly for the more serious offence of bribing the local sergeant. However, she did manage to educate all her children privately and marry three daughters into the aristocracy. She once had the distinction (and good sense) to refuse to cash a large cheque for one of the 43 Club's most notorious members, Clarence Hatry (see page 47).

Opposite the 43 Club, Chinese businessman and drug dealer 'Brilliant' Chang, real name Chan Nan, a 1920s Soho figure as notorious as Mrs Meyrick, ran the Palm Court Club, where he purveyed cocaine and heroin mainly to young women, whom he is said to have deliberately converted into addicts. Following a raid on his Limehouse hideaway, he was arrested in 1924, imprisoned for 14 months, and then deported.

Carry on to the end of Gerrard Street. The Latin Quarter night-club, where David Knight was killed, was down Wardour Street to your left, on the far side at No 13. The Knights had gone to the club to find Johnny Isaacs, who had taken part in an attack on David at a pub in Islington. Isaacs wasn't there but Zomparelli was. A fight started and Knight was stabbed to death. It later turned out that the club had been paying protection money to him.

Turn right into Wardour Street. On the right is Dansey Place. Between the world wars there was a cast-iron urinal here which was the most notorious 'cottage' (gay men's meeting place) in the West End. Called Clarkson's Cottage, after Willy Clarkson's theatrical costume shop across the road (the building with the clock on the front), it was a popular target for blackmailing gangs. Shortly after World War I a wealthy habitué is said to have been taken for £100,000. After World War II an American with fond memories bought Clarkson's Cottage and re-erected it in the grounds of his country house outside New York. It may still be there.

Continue to the end of Wardour Street, cross Shaftesbury Avenue and turn left. When you get to Rupert Street turn right and walk up to the junction with Brewer Street. You are now in the centre of modern Soho's licensed sex trade. Comparatively tame and small-scale compared with what it was in the 1970s, it consists mainly of a few sex shops, peep shows, strip clubs and video outlets. In Walker's Court, ahead, is one of the oldest and certainly the most famous of Soho's strip clubs, The Raymond Revuebar, opened in April 1958 by 33-year-old Paul Raymond. In the 1960s the club made Raymond a fortune, enabling him to move into magazine publishing (titles like *Men Only* and *Club International*) and property in the 1970s; in 1990 he bought *Mayfair*, another well known men's magazine. Today Raymond owns much of Soho, including most of Brewer Street, and is said to be worth some £350m, making him the 43rd richest person in the country. Not bad for the son of a Liverpool lorry driver and former variety performer with a mind-reading act.

Walk through Walker's Court and cross Peter Street into Berwick Street. Somewhere here in 1751 Mrs Jane Goadby opened a brand new kind of brothel, different from anything then on offer in London. Based on the best Paris establishments, which were a cut above their rivals across the Channel, it featured beautiful and healthy girls dressed in fine clothes and presented in luxury surroundings suitable for the high-class clientele. A house surgeon was on hand to ensure that the girls remained in the peak of condition. Mrs Goadby prospered, expanding into a neighbouring house in 1754 and moving to grander premises in nearby Great Marlborough Street in 1760. After three decades as a madam she is said to have retired on the profits of her trade to a fine house in the country.

When you get to Broadwick Street (✠ left), turn right and then first left into Wardour Street. The modern shop-and-office building on the left stands on the site of 153 Wardour Street, where on 10 February 1942 ex-actress Nita Ward was found dead in her flat. Her throat had been slashed and her body mutilated with a tin-opener. In succeeding days two other women were murdered in the West End, both strangled and mutilated with a razor. Two of these three women were prostitutes. That fact, plus the mutilations, led to fears that another Jack the Ripper was on the loose. For some time Soho prostitutes went in fear of their lives, until eventually police linked RAF cadet George Cummins, arrested for an attack on a woman outside a pub, with the murders. He was executed on 25 June 1942 for the murder of four women.

Carry on up Wardour Street. It was at the All Nighters Club in this street (the club is not listed in the phone books or directories of the time, so it has not been possible to establish its precise location) that two Notting Hill criminals, Lucky Gordon and Johnny Edgecombe, had a fight over Christine Keeler, an ex-girlfriend of both men, in the early hours of 28 October 1962. Gordon's badly slashed face required 17 stitches. This was the first in a series of incidents which culminated in the notorious Profumo Affair seven months later (more details on page 147).

At the end of Wardour Street, cross Oxford Street into Berners Street. Ahead, on the right, the entrance to the Berners Hotel's Reflections restaurant stands on the site of 6 Berners Street, where the bank of Marsh, Sibbald and Co was based from its foundation in 1782. When one of the bank's major customers went bankrupt in 1815, managing partner Henry Fauntleroy illegally sold other customers' stocks and shares in order to keep the bank afloat. Having discovered how easy fraud was, he carried on, using it to fund his secret life as a keeper of mistresses. One of these was the notorious woman-of-pleasure Mary Bertram, otherwise known as Mrs Bang. Because Fauntleroy continued to pay out dividends, his crime went undetected until 1824, by which time many small tradesmen and others had been ruined. After a sensational trial, he was hanged for forgery at Newgate on 30 November 1824 in front of a crowd estimated at 100,000.

Just beyond the Berners Hotel you come to Eastcastle Street, the scene of the robbery at 4.17am on 21 May 1952, when Billy Hill's gang hijacked a Post Office mail van carrying money from Paddington railway station to St Martin's-Le-Grand post office in the City. Meticulously planned and executed with ruthless efficiency, it netted £287,000, making Hill a wealthy man and heralding the start of what was called 'project crime'. Until another similar crime nine years later – the much more famous and lucrative Great Train Robbery – the Great Mail Van Robbery of 1952 was the biggest robbery in British criminal history.

Cross Eastcastle Street and carry on along Berners Street. The huge Sanderson building on the left covers the site of 54 Berners Street, scene of the 19th century's most notorious hoax. After he had bet his friend Samuel Beazley that he could make any quite ordinary London address the most talked about in the city, practical joker Theodore Hook decided to make an example of 54 Berners Street, the home of Mrs Tottenham, a lady who had somehow offended him. Over a period of six weeks he wrote some 4000 letters asking all manner of tradesmen, professionals and public figures to call on Mrs Tottenham on a certain day in November 1809. On the day in question, Berners Street was packed all day long with a dense throng of horses, carts and people all trying to get to No 54. The Governor of the Bank of England was among them, as were the Lord Mayor of London, the Chairman of the East India Company, the Archbishop of Canterbury and the royal Duke of Gloucester. Then, at 5.00pm, responding to ads in the papers, hundreds of unemployed servants arrived seeking positions. It took the police until late at night to clear up the confusion. The hoax duly made 54 Berners Street the talk of the capital, and Hook of course won his bet.

Continue along Berners Street. At the top, turn right into Mortimer Street, then left into Cleveland Street, and walk along to the junction with

Tottenham Street. On the left, the private wing (Woolavington Wing) of the Middlesex Hospital stands on the site of 19 Cleveland Street. In 1889 when it was a male brothel this address became the focal point of the most notorious homosexual scandal of the Victorian era. Following a theft investigation at a City post office, it was discovered that telegraph boys from the office were being paid 'for going to bed with gentlemen' at the brothel. These gentlemen apparently included Lord Arthur Somerset, son of the Duke of Beaufort and an intimate of the Prince of Wales, Lord Euston, son of the Duke of Grafton, and a Colonel Jervoise. Suspicion also hovered around the Prince of Wales's eldest son, Prince Eddy. The *North London Press* subsequently got hold of the story, claiming that the brothel proprietor had been allowed to escape and two of the boys had been given relatively mild prison sentences in order to cover up the scandal and its connection with the royal family. Lord Arthur Somerset retired into self-imposed exile on the French Riviera, where he remained until his death in 1930, but Lord Euston stayed and successfully sued for libel. The paper's editor was jailed for a year.

Turn right into Tottenham Street and walk to the junction with Charlotte Street. The Margaret Pyke Centre on the left corner stands where Jay's the Jewellers was in 1947. Three armed robbers held it up on 29 April that year. Staff foiled the robbery and the gang fled on foot, their getaway car having been blocked in by a lorry. A father of six, 34-year-old Alex de Antiquis, drove his motorcycle in front of them to try to stop them, but was fatally shot in the head for his pains. The three robbers were subsequently sentenced to death, but one was too young to hang. Of the two executed, one – 23-year-old Harry Jenkins – was involved in, but not charged with, the death of Captain Binney in 1944 (see page 55). On this occasion Jenkins did not fire the fatal shot, but he was hanged nonetheless, partly to discourage the increasing use of firearms in the underworld. The underworld duly got the message, and police began finding discarded guns all over the place.

Opposite the Margaret Pyke Centre, 64 Charlotte Street (the Hogarth Studios) was – or at least an earlier building on the site was – once the most notorious flagellation brothel in London. Opened by Mrs Theresa Berkeley in 1828, it was a place where you could be whipped, beaten, pricked, curry-combed, scrubbed and half-strangled to your heart's content if you so desired – provided, of course, you had the wherewithal. Mrs B's particular claim to fame, and the source of her substantial and quickly acquired fortune, was the Berkeley Horse, a frame on which clients were spreadeagled to allow more efficient scourging. After her death in 1836, the Horse, bizarrely, was donated to the Society for the Promotion of the Arts, Manufacture and Commerce in the Adelphi (now called the

RSA), one of whose members was pornographer George Cannon, a specialist in flagellant literature.

Now turn right into Charlotte Street. Cross Goodge Street. Turn right into Rathbone Street and follow it round to the left. When you get to the Newman Arms pub, on the right, go through the archway into Newman Passage and turn left when you come out on Newman Street. Towards the end of the 18th century, as more and more of the West End was developed, many prostitutes moved west to Marylebone, 'the new grand paradise of love', and in particular to Newman Street. *Harris's List* for 1793 described one Newman Street whore, a Miss H—rington, as 'a knowing one about twenty-five, with a tolerable good complexion, in company chatty, witty and agreeable'. When you entered her room she immediately took you to a sofa and showed you her 'haven of delight' – 'in return she likewise expects a view of nature's gifts from you, which if she thinks clean and properly adapted, she will unload for two pounds two'.

Walk on down to Oxford Street, cross over and turn left. The building at Nos 55–59 Oxford Street, on the east corner of Soho Street, has intimate connections with two notorious doctors, Talbot Bridgewater and Hawley Crippen. Bridgewater housed here both his medical practice and an elaborate forgery factory staffed by several well known members of the criminal fraternity. The factory specialized in stealing things like cheques and postal orders (for example, by breaking open pillar boxes) and then forging increased values on them before cashing them in. Police discovered the factory in 1905 and Bridgewater went to prison for seven years. While he was serving his sentence, dentist Crippen worked as a partner in the Yale Tooth Specialist Company at the same address. Having fallen in love with one of the company's typists, Ethel Le Neve, he murdered his unpleasant wife and buried her under the coal cellar of their house in Holloway. After a dramatic chase across the Atlantic by a Scotland Yard detective, Crippen was arrested. He was executed in 1910. Ethel Le Neve later married an accountant, and died in 1967.

Continue on along Oxford Street to Tottenham Court Road station, where the walk ends.

Mayfair and St James's

High-Society Gambling

St James's and Mayfair were developed as upper-class residential districts in the late 17th and 18th centuries respectively. Only since World War II have they been increasingly taken over by business. The upper classes have always lived by their own rules so it is not surprising to find many notorious sites in these two West End enclaves – so many, in fact, that the bulk of this chapter has had to be given over to them. The introduction, which is accordingly shorter than in other chapters, focuses on the one thing which made St James's notorious in the late 18th and early 19th centuries – the upper-class craze for gambling, pursued in the gentlemen's clubs which were then becoming a feature of the area. One MP of the time referred to these clubs – some of which still survive, though their existence is now rather more sedate – as the 'abominable nurseries of gambling in St James's Street which are the bane of our young men of rank'.

Gambling in St James's

Gambling took root in the rich and idle upper classes in the Restoration era, and then gradually spread out from London and down through the social ranks until it came to obsess the whole country from the early 18th century onwards. In mid-century the government tried to stamp it out, but succeeded only in driving the vice out of sight into private houses, gambling hells (so called because they were full of lost souls) and private clubs.

St James's was full of hells and private clubs, but it was the aristocratic clubs that became particularly notorious, because it was here that the biggest sums were lost and won. The most outrageous clubs on this account were White's, Almack's and the Cocoa Tree. White's was (and still is, as you will see on the walk) in St James's Street, but the Cocoa Tree and Almack's were in Pall Mall. Huge fortunes in money, houses and land – representing millions of pounds in today's money – were lost and won virtually every day in these clubs on the throw of a dice or the turn of a card. At White's, whist, a game of skill, was particularly popular, but the other clubs – particularly Almack's, which became Brooks's in 1778 when it moved to its current position in St James's Street – tended to go more for games of chance like faro and hazard; these involved cards and dice respectively.

At Almack's, on the site of modern 49–51 Pall Mall, the play was especially fast and furious. 'The young men of the age lose five, ten, fifteen thousand pounds in an evening there,' wrote Horace Walpole in 1770. 'Lord Stavordale, not one and twenty, lost £11,000 there last Tuesday but recovered it by one great hand at hazard: he swore a great oath – "Now, if I had been playing deep, I might have won millions!"'

Stavordale's cousin, Charles James Fox, was probably the most notorious gambler of the era. A founder member of Almack's at the age of 16, Fox had been introduced to gambling as a boy by his father, who gave him five guineas a night to try out on the tables. Let loose in the West End in the 1770s, by which time he was about the same age as Stavordale, he went completely wild. In one week in February 1772, for example, he played hazard at Almack's from Tuesday evening until 5.00pm on Wednesday, losing £11,000. On Thursday he made a less than usually scintillating speech in the House of Commons (despite his youth Fox was already an MP, with a reputation as a speaker). Having dined at 11.30 that evening, he went to White's and drank until 7.00 the next morning. Then he went to Almack's again, this time winning £6000. At 3.00 that afternoon he set off for Newmarket to blow the morning's winnings at the races. Returning to London a couple of days later, he lost a further £10,000. Meanwhile his elder brother Stephen had also lost £11,000 at the tables. So between them the two brothers, both in their early 20s, lost in less than a week a total of £32,000, a gigantic sum in terms of today's money.

In 1774, when his parents and his elder brother died, Fox was besieged by creditors demanding payment. Well over £100,000 was forked out by the family estate to settle with them. But even this fantastic sum was not enough to wipe out all his liabilities. For example, his schoolfriend and fellow gambler, Lord Carlisle, who had acted as security for some of Fox's loans, found himself obliged to pay £2000 a year in interest payments on Fox's behalf. This was one-sixth of Carlisle's income, which meant he had to give up his London house and retrench heavily at his country seat in Yorkshire.

Despite the magnitude of Fox's crash, it did not deter him from gambling. Throughout the rest of the 1770s and into the 1780s he carried on in the same old way, getting money where he could (even from the waiters at Brooks's) and losing it just as fast. He was able to live like this only because he was totally indifferent to the consequences, both for himself and for his friends. One night when he had lost another huge sum, a friend went round to Fox's lodgings in St James's Street half expecting to find him with a pistol in his hand. Instead, Fox was ensconced in an armchair calmly reading Herodotus. 'What better employment for a man who has lost his last shilling,' wrote the friend.

Eventually Fox's friends clubbed together and raised enough money to pay off his new debts and provide him with an income which he could not gamble away. He was lucky. For many of his contemporaries the gambling addiction had disastrous, sometimes fatal, consequences. Actor Thomas King lost his savings and house in the 1780s. Banker George Drummond lost £20,000 on the only occasion he played whist at White's and had to resign from the family bank. Henry Weston, the 23-year-old nephew of Admiral Sir Hugh Palliser, resorted to forgery to pay his gambling debts; forgery was then a capital offence, and so he went to the gallows in 1796. Several other gambling debtors – including Sir John Bland and Lord Montfort – killed themselves after losing their entire properties. After a last evening playing whist at White's, Lord Montfort got up the next morning, summoned his lawyer, made his will, checked that it would not be invalidated by suicide, and shot himself before his lawyer was even out of the front door.

The most famous case of gambling suicide involved John Damer, son of Lord Milton and heir to £30,000 a year. In 1776 Damer lost £40,000 to notorious gamester 'Captain' Dick England, who made it his business to ruin those he played with. When his father refused to pay his debts, Damer went to the Bedford Arms Coffee House in Covent Garden, summoned a blind fiddler, enjoyed himself with some prostitutes, and then shot himself. Damer's death made a profound impression on society, but it didn't stop people gambling.

Though most were losers at the tables of St James's, a fortunate few won. General Scott, father-in-law of statesman George Canning, won £200,000 during a long career of successful whist-playing. Henry Thynne, who once resigned from Almack's in disgust because he had won 'only' £12,000 in two months, later returned to the St James's gambling fray and won enough to pay off all his debts and buy a house. And Lord Robert Spencer, who lost every penny of the fortune given him by his brother the Duke of Marlborough, as a last resort borrowed some money, set up a faro bank at Brooks's and won £100,000. He used the money to buy an estate in Sussex and never gambled again.

A final instance of good fortune among gamblers concerns a Mr Harvey, who in 1780 lost £100,000 to Irish gamester Mr O'Birne at the Cocoa Tree Club (on the site of modern 46 Pall Mall). Instead of making him sell his estate to pay the debt, O'Birne took pity on Harvey – perhaps because he was young and had only just inherited his property – and kept just £10,000, offering Harvey the chance to play again for the other £90,000. Having nothing to lose, Harvey took it – and won.

Gambling died down in the West End in the 1790s, but broke out again with renewed intensity in the early 19th century. Watier's, founded in 1805 by the Prince Regent's chef as a completely new type of club, where fine

French cuisine replaced the usual stodgy British fare dished up at places like White's and Brooks's, rapidly became a favourite gambling club, with dandy Beau Brummell setting the pace until his retirement to the Continent in 1816 to escape his creditors. His fate was a lesson to his fellow members: the gambling at Watier's was just *too* destructive, and the club closed in 1819.

Nine years later the upper-class gambling craze in St James's reached its apogee with the opening of Crockford's, at 50 St James's Street. Whereas all the other clubs were primarily social and political gatherings with gambling attached, Crockford's was founded specifically for gambling by a professional gambler. Nevertheless, it was also a fine club – in fact, by far the most opulent and best-equipped club yet seen in London. Former fishmonger William Crockford knew he had to provide the best possible facilities – including fine French food and wine, all included in the annual subscription, which was the highest in London – if he were to succeed in his aim, which was to make as much money as possible out of the richest members of London's high society. Mainly using hazard, which gave the house an average 15% advantage, he succeeded brilliantly. Already rich when he started the club – the capital allegedly came from £100,000 won at a single 24-hour sitting – he is said to have made a fortune of £1.2m, equivalent, according to one observer, to the whole of the ready money of the then existing generation of the aristocracy. Old Crocky retired to his palatial home in Carlton House Terrace in 1840 and died there four years later.

It was at about this time that a combination of Victorian repression and anti-gambling legislation finally stamped out the gambling craze that had beset St James's for the best part of seventy years.

THE MAYFAIR AND ST JAMES'S WALK

Start:	Piccadilly underground station (Piccadilly and Bakerloo lines).
Finish:	Marble Arch underground station (Central line).
Length:	2¾ miles (4.4km).
Refreshments:	Shepherd Market, a little enclave of largely pedestrianized streets with pubs, take-aways and restaurants, some with open-air seating, is at the halfway stage, and is therefore the obvious place to stop. But there are also plenty of places around the underground stations at the start and finish of the walk.

From Piccadilly station (♈) take the 'Lower Regent Street Eros' exit and walk straight on down the left-hand side of Regent Street (the 'Lower' is not part of the street name any more). The junction with Charles II Street

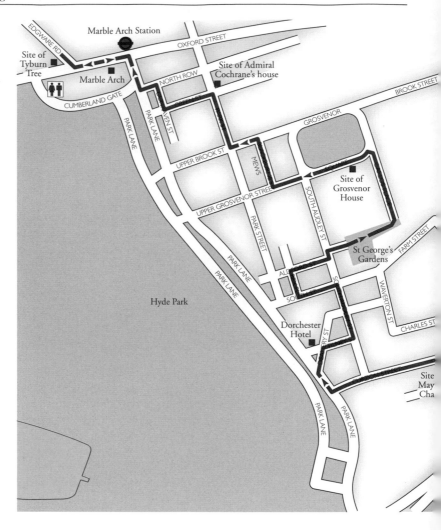

is the approximate site of the White Lion tavern where, on the evening of 19 July 1822, 57-year-old Percy Jocelyn, an Irish bishop and son of an earl, was caught with a young soldier from one of the Guards regiments in an upstairs private room. Jocelyn, dressed in his episcopal garb, tried desperately to escape but was rather hampered by the fact that his breeches were round his ankles. Having been taken to nearby Vine Street watch-house, he later jumped bail and worked as a butler in Edinburgh under an assumed name before dying there incognito in 1843.

Turn left into Charles II Street and, halfway along, cross right into the Royal Opera Arcade. In 1825, when the arcade surrounded all four sides

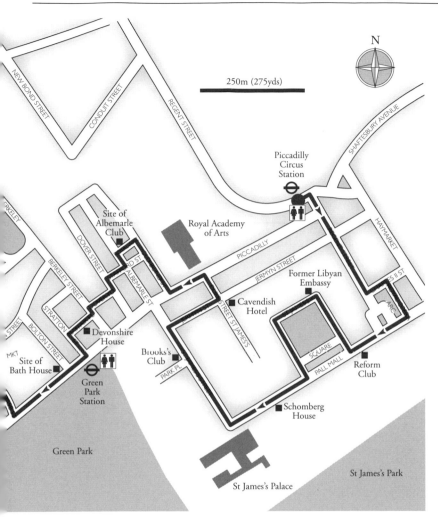

of the opera house, now Her Majesty's Theatre, bookseller Joseph Stockdale, based at 24 Opera Colonnade, as it was called then, caused a sensation when he published in instalments the scandalous memoirs of Harriette Wilson, the most successful society prostitute in Regency London. Harriette had had many well known lovers, and all were mentioned except those who had paid £200 to have their names omitted. When he received his blackmail demand, the Duke of Wellington responded with characteristic acerbity: 'Publish and be damned.' Harriette did just that, and people queued ten deep to be the first to read the Wellington instalment.

At the far end of the arcade you emerge on Pall Mall. Here, on 12 February 1682, while driving home from dinner, landowner Tom Thynne was ambushed in his coach by three men and shot dead. The assailants were later hanged on the spot, but the man widely believed to be behind the killing, Count Charles Königsmarck, known to be jealous of Thynne's immensely rich heiress wife, was acquitted, which sparked a public outcry. However, the count was killed in battle four years later, so perhaps justice was done in a way. The mystery surrounding the count's involvement has made the case a notorious murder whodunnit ever since.

Turn right on Pall Mall and cross Waterloo Place. The third building on the left, looking like a grand Italian palace, is the Reform Club. It was here in February 1856 that City swindler John Sadleir (see page 41) came to write two suicide notes before going up to Hampstead Heath and swallowing poison. One of them was a confession to his solicitor: 'I cannot live. I have ruined too many. I could not live and see that agony.' Turn right opposite the Reform Club into St James's Square and walk up to the top right-hand corner. Facing you, No 5 was the Libyan embassy in 1984 when, on 17 April, Yvonne Fletcher, a policewoman controlling an anti-Gaddafi demonstration, was shot dead by a sudden burst of gunfire from an upper-storey window. Her murderer, shielded by diplomatic immunity, was never brought to book, but in 1999 the Libyans effectively admitted culpability by paying Yvonne's family £250,000 in compensation, after which diplomatic relations between Libya and Britain resumed. There is a memorial to Yvonne across the road, by the garden railings.

Turn left now along the north side of the square and then left again down its west side. Foreign Secretary Lord Castlereagh used to live on the near corner of King Street. Castlereagh was not above resorting to the odd prostitute on his nocturnal strolls home from Westminster. Once the girl turned out to be a man, part of a blackmail set-up. After the Irish bishop affair of July 1822, mentioned at the start of the walk, Castlereagh was desperately afraid that he too would be exposed (in his case falsely) as a homosexual. So, while the balance of his mind was severely disturbed, he cut his throat at his country home in Kent on 12 August 1822. A sad end to a gifted politician.

Cross King Street. On the right a predecessor of the present No 21 was where the Duke of York installed Arabella Churchill and later, after he had succeeded to the throne as James II, Katherine Sedley, two of his many mistresses. The latter stayed until 1696, by which time her royal lover had been an exile in France for several years.

Continue out of the square into Pall Mall and turn right. On the left, the central part of Schomberg House, at 80–82 Pall Mall, was home in the 1780s to notorious quack Dr James Graham's Temple of Health and Hymen. A kind of sex clinic, the temple featured the Celestial Bed, which the gullible paid large fees to use since it was supposed to guarantee conception. One of Graham's nubile assistants and mud-bath demonstrators was Emma Hart, who later became the famous Lady Hamilton, Lord Nelson's mistress. Graham, not surprisingly, ended his days in a lunatic asylum, having become a religious fanatic.

Next door to Schomberg House, the original 79 Pall Mall was the house Charles II gave to his most famous mistress, Nell Gwynn (see page 137). She was, as she described herself, the 'Protestant whore', a dig at Charles's French Catholic mistress, Louise de Kéroualle. Having insisted that Charles give her the freehold of the house (which is why it is now the only non-Crown Estate property on the south side of Pall Mall), Nell lived here until her death in 1687 at the age of just 37.

On this side of the road Nos 45 and 48 mark the sites of, respectively, Almack's and the Cocoa Tree, two of the notorious gaming clubs mentioned in the introduction. A little further on, a covered entrance leads into Angel Court. Just this side of it, a similar narrow alley called Pall Mall Place has recently been built over. In the mid 18th century, when it was called King's Place, this was home to the King's Place Nunneries, the West End's most notorious enclave of brothels. Former prostitute Charlotte Hayes ran the most famous of them, The Cloisters, an upmarket establishment rivalling Mrs Goadby's pioneering house of ill-fame in Soho (see page 116).

Beyond Angel Court you pass Quadrant House (55–58 Pall Mall), where between 1879 and 1912 City swindler Horatio Bottomley (see page 46) entertained his mistresses in a luxury flat. Over on the left, venerable St James's Palace was the scene of a grisly incident in June 1810 when the Duke of Cumberland suffered severe head wounds and his valet Joseph Sellis was found dead in bed. The official story was that Sellis had killed himself after attempting to assassinate the duke. But rumour had it that Sellis had been killed, possibly by the duke, to cover up some sexual scandal, possibly homosexual. The fact that Sellis, whose throat had been cut, was found with his cravat still in place around his neck tended to lend credence to the murder theory.

Walk on to the end of Pall Mall and turn right into St James's Street, walking up the left-hand side. Halfway up on the left, Park Place was home to the brothel kept by Elizabeth Needham, the most notorious madam in early 18th century London and one of the real-life characters featured in William Hogarth's series *A Harlot's Progress*. For keeping 'a lewd and disorderly house' Mrs Needham was sentenced to stand in the pillory twice here at the entrance to Park Place in April 1731, but when she appeared for the first time she was so badly injured that she did not survive for the second. The grand building on the north corner of Park Place is

Brooks's Club, here since 1778 and another of the 18th century gambling clubs mentioned in the introduction to this chapter. Brooks's started out as Almack's in Pall Mall in 1764.

Continue up St James's Street as far as Bennet Street. Ahead, on the right, the building with the ground-floor bay window is White's Club, Brooks's main rival as a gambling club in the 18th century. Now use the crossing to get over to the entrance to Jermyn Street and look back to the large building on the west side of St James's Street, opposite White's. This is the former Devonshire Club, successor to Crockford's, where William Crockford emptied the pockets of a whole generation of the upper classes between 1828 and 1844. (Both White's and Crockford's are described in this chapter's introduction.) Continue on into Jermyn Street. Somewhere in this street, in her brother's betting shop and illicit gambling den (whose precise location I have been unable to identify), Shirley Pitts, so-called Queen of Shoplifters in the 1960s, stashed her loot and changed her disguise so that she could continue to trawl the West End stores unrecognized.

At the junction with Duke Street St James's you can see to the right the Cavendish Hotel, made famous by Rosa Lewis, the so-called Duchess of Duke Street. Rosa's services included the sexual initiation of well born young men and the provision of 'nice clean tarts, dear' for officers home on leave during World War I.

Turn left into Duke Street St James's. Cross Piccadilly, turn left and then turn right when you get to Old Bond Street. In May 1876 Agnew's, on the left at No 43, suffered the 19th century's most sensational art theft when the notorious Adam Worth, the greatest thief of the age, stole the most expensive English picture of the day, Gainsborough's portrait of Georgiana, Duchess of Devonshire. Worth was unable to dispose of the picture, however, and was eventually forced to return it 25 years later for an undisclosed sum through Pinkerton's detective agency. It hangs today in the Metropolitan Museum of Art in New York.

A little further on, the house at Nos 37–38 in the early 19th century was the home of successful landscape painter Olive Serres, who bizarrely claimed to be a royal princess. Probably slightly mad, she got into serious debt trying to prove her claim, as a result of which she spent 13 years living in the Rules of the King's Bench (see page 24) before her death in 1834.

Carry on along Old Bond Street and turn left into the Royal Arcade. Emerge on Albemarle Street. No 13, just to the right, is the site of the Albemarle Club, where on 18 February 1895 Lord Queensberry left his famous card for Oscar Wilde bearing the fatal words 'posing as a somdomite' (he meant 'sodomite'). Queensberry was the father of Wilde's

Plate 28: *The north-east corner of St James's Square where policewoman Yvonne Fletcher was shot dead in 1984 (see page 126).*

Plate 29: *Lily Langtry, famous actress and mistress of the Prince of Wales (see pages 84 and 133).*

Plate 30: *A hanging at Tyburn. The three-cornered Tyburn Tree is at the back on the right, next to Mother Proctor's Pews (see pages 29 and 134).*

Plate 31: *The Who's wildman drummer Keith Moon overdosed in Mayfair the day after getting engaged to his girlfriend, Annette Walter-Lax (see page 131).*

Plate 32: *Oscar Wilde, left, and his lover, Lord Alfred Douglas (see page 128).*

Plate 33: *Nell Gwynn, the best-known of Charles II's many mistresses (see pages 85, 127 and 137).*

Plate 34: *Deranged merchant John Bellingham shoots Prime Minister Spencer Perceval in the lobby of the House of Commons in 1812 (see page 142).*

Plate 35: *Mandy Rice-Davies and Christine Keeler, the two girls at the heart of the notorious Profumo Affair of 1963 (see pages 116 and 147).*

Plate 36: *Old Palace Yard, Westminster, where Gunpowder Plotter Guy Fawkes was executed in 1606 (see page 142).*

Plate 37: *Donald Maclean, Guy Burgess and Kim Philby, three notorious Soviet spies of the 1950s and 1960s (see pages 143 and 149).*

lover, Lord Alfred Douglas. As all the world knows, Wilde unwisely prosecuted Queensberry for libel, lost and was then himself arrested on a charge of indecent conduct and sent to prison.

Turn left on Albemarle Street and then first right into Stafford Street. The two buildings at the end on the left (Nos 7 and 7A) were used as brothels in the 1940s by the notorious Messina vice gang (see page 107). Duncan Webb, the journalist whose investigations led to the break-up of the gang, collected 28 Messina addresses altogether, most of them in Mayfair.

Turn left into Dover Street. Go through the archway on the right into Dover Yard and out onto Berkeley Street. No 9, just to your right, was once the home of Elizabeth Howard, one of Harriet Wilson's successors as a society prostitute in the 19th century. Having worked her way up through the social ranks to become the lover of Louis Napoleon in 1846, she lent him a large sum of money that helped him return to France and eventually, following the 1848 revolution, become Emperor Napoleon III. Elizabeth followed her lover across the Channel, where she was amply rewarded with cash and the title Comtesse de Beauregard.

Cross Berkeley Street into Mayfair Place, passing the rear of a modern office block called Devonshire House. In the 18th century the dukes of Devonshire had their town house here: the 5th duke lived in a notorious ménage à trois with his duchess (the subject of the Gainsborough portrait stolen from Agnew's) and Lady Elizabeth Foster, the duchess's best friend. The duke had children by both women, and the duchess had a couple more by Lord Grey.

When you get to Stratton Street, turn left and then right onto Piccadilly (⚲ in Green Park subway). The building on the near corner of Bolton Street (No 81) stands on the site of Watier's, the early-19th century gambling club mentioned in the introduction. During the 1920s the opposite corner of Bolton Street was occupied by Bath House. One night in June 1924 thieves broke in and stole part of Sir Julius Wernher's antique jewel collection, escaping via a window and rear fire escape. Such was the huge value of the haul — £500,000 is one figure quoted — that the audacious robbery is said to have sparked off a London cat-burglary craze that lasted about a decade.

Carry on along Piccadilly and cross Half Moon Street. Charlotte Hayes — encountered earlier as proprietress of one of the brothels in King's Place, in St James's — lived in style on her ill-gotten gains in the corner house here with her equally notorious husband, Colonel Dennis O'Kelly, an Irish adventurer who started life as a sedan-chairman and ended up owning the 18th century's most famous racehorse. He died here in 1787; she died mad in 1811.

The next building, set back from the road, was the home of Lord Palmerston when, as Prime Minister and in his late 70s, he was cited in 1863 in a sensational divorce case. Mayfair at that time, as Henry James once wrote, lived for the next divorce. With his usual skill Palmerston managed to extricate himself on a technicality, and so avoided having to pay the £20,000 damages claimed by the Irish journalist with whose former-governess wife he was alleged to have had an affair.

A few steps further on, turn right into White Horse Street. At the far end you come to Shepherd Market. Dating from the late 17th century, this former market area has long been a red-light district, and today is one of the few places in the West End where you can still sometimes see prostitutes soliciting, especially on a warm summer's evening. The situation is very different, though, from what it was in the 1970s when in just one year (1977) 2200 prostitutes were arrested or cautioned in Shepherd Market and nearby Park Lane, four times the number in all Soho. In the 1940s the Messinas could be seen here almost every evening, doing the rounds of their girls and collecting their takings.

Turn left into Shepherd Street. In Carrington Street, on the left, society prostitute Kitty Fisher operated from 1759 to 1765 (hers was the fifth house along the street on the right-hand side). She charged 100 guineas a night and slept only with the best. When the Duke of York (a younger brother of George III) gave her a £50 note claiming it was all he had on him at the time, it's said she showed her contempt for his mean-ness by clapping the money between two slices of bread and eating it!

Now turn right into Trebeck Street and then left when you get to Curzon Street. Immediately on the left, No 38A (opposite Crewe House and between Trebeck and Hertford Streets) is the site of the Mayfair Chapel, where from the 1730s former Fleet parson Alexander Keith celebrated clandestine marriages without banns or licences. When the local parish church complained, Dr Keith was excommunicated and sent to the Fleet prison. Nothing daunted, he simply arranged for a new chapel to open next to the original one and staffed it with four paid clerics. He also resumed work as a Fleet parson. Despite performing over 7000 marriage ceremonies at a guinea a time during his career, he was still in the debtors' prison when he died in 1758, four years after Fleet marriages had been made illegal by the 1754 Marriage Act (see page 35).

Carry on along Curzon Street. In the late 1960s the street was made notorious by the so-called Curzon Street Cowboys, young guardsmen and cavalry troopers carrying on the age-old tradition of hiring themselves out as rent-boys to supplement their meagre army pay (rather like Private John Moverly, the young guardsman caught with the Bishop of Clogher in the

White Lion tavern, as described at the start of the walk). The police soon stamped out the trade because homosexuality was a still a military offence at this time, even though it had recently been legalized in civilian life. At 30 Curzon Street you pass Crockford's, a modern version of – but no relation to – the old gaming club.

Towards the far end of Curzon Street you come to Curzon Place. The Who's wildman drummer, Keith Moon, responsible for many notorious incidents – such as putting explosive charges in his drumkit and leaving live piranha fish in hotel bathrooms – died in a fourth-floor flat here on 7 September 1977, the day after he had become engaged. Ironically, he overdosed on pills prescribed to treat his alcoholism.

At the end of Curzon Street, turn right into Park Lane. Cross the entrance to Stanhope Gate (City swindler Clarence Hatry – see page 47 – lived at No 5, three buildings to the right on the right-hand side of the street) and branch right into Deanery Street, passing the Dorchester Hotel. It was as he was leaving the hotel after a diplomatic dinner that Shlomo Argov, the Israeli ambassador, was gunned down by the Arab assassin Ghassov Said on 3 June 1982. Argov survived but was paralysed from the neck down.

The original Dorchester House was the town house of the libertine 3rd Marquess of Hertford, a notorious Regency rake and the model for the loathsome Lord Steyne in Thackeray's novel *Vanity Fair* (1847–8). Hertford's house had a discreet back entrance leading to a little cottage in the garden where he entertained his numerous mistresses and the prostitutes procured for him by his French valet, Nicholas Suisse. Harriette Wilson (see page 125) was one of his regular companions.

Turn first right into Tilney Street and walk to the end, facing the lamp-post across the road in Audley Square. Following his defection to the West, former KGB man Oleg Gordievsky revealed that, during the Cold War, Soviet spies had a complicated series of message systems involving chalkmarks on this lamp-post and on the back of one of the benches in nearby St George's Gardens (see below). The chalkmarks indicated that the spy had dropped material in the dead-letter box at Brompton Oratory or Holy Trinity Church, both in Knightsbridge, and that the KGB support had successfully collected the material. With all the resources of the Soviet Union at their command, one would have thought they could have come up with a more efficient system of communication than this.

Turn left into South Audley Street and then take the second left into South Street. After shooting the Israeli ambassador, 22-year-old Ghassov Said, a member of the Al-Asifa terrorist group, ran off into South Street. He was pursued by Colin Simpson, the ambassador's Special Branch bodyguard. After Said's machine-pistol jammed Simpson managed to wing him and bring him down. Said was subsequently sentenced, along with two accomplices arrested later in Brixton, to a lengthy term of imprisonment.

Further along on the right, 15 South Street bears a plaque to Catherine Walters, perhaps the best-known of half a dozen or so leading society prostitutes in mid-Victorian London. Better known as Skittles – she once worked in a skittle alley in a slum public house – she made her name in the 1860s in the Argyll Rooms (see page 92) and in Hyde Park, where she was paid by a Mayfair livery stable to advertise its horseflesh, reputedly in a skintight costume without underwear. Skittles came here in her early 30s and stayed for the rest of her life, entertaining Prime Minister William Gladstone and other respectable notables at her regular salons.

Turn right into Rex Place and then first right into Aldford Place. Cross South Audley Street and go to the left of the Grosvenor Chapel into St George's Gardens; it was on the back of a bench here that the Soviets made chalkmarks as part of their extraordinarily cumbersome communications system involving the Audley Square lamp-post.

Walk straight through the garden and exit left at the far end. Cross Mount Street. Walk up Carlos Place to Grosvenor Square and turn left. No 45, the third door on the left, is the site of Lord Grosvenor's town house in the 18th century. In 1769 Lady Grosvenor was discovered in a passionate affair with the 'weak and debauched' Duke of Cumberland. Lord Grosvenor, himself no saint, promptly sued the duke for £10,000 damages and won. Because of the scale of the award (a huge sum for the time) and the duke's royal connections (he was another brother of George III), the case became one of the most sensational in a century of similar sensations and the avidly read trial report went into five editions. No wonder, when it contained such details as the fact that Lady Grosvenor was found with the duke in a room at an inn 'with her dress unbuttoned and her breasts wholly exposed'. Lady Grosvenor was banned from Grosvenor House, and the duke, after a dalliance with a timber merchant's wife, married a widow called Mrs Horton.

Further along this side of the square the Britannia Hotel, built in 1967, covers Nos 44 and 40 Grosvenor Square. In February 1820 conspirators led by Arthur Thistlewood planned to attack No 44 with hand-grenades and kill the entire Cabinet while its members were dining with Lord Harrowby, whose town house it was. However, the plot, hatched nearby in a hayloft in Cato Street, Marylebone, was foiled and Thistlewood and four others were hanged and decapitated at Newgate (see page 38). Nearly half a century earlier, No 40 was the London home of the recently widowed Countess of Strathmore and her new husband, Captain Andrew Stoney, a particularly nasty piece of work. Over a period of ten years, during which they lived at both 40 and 28 Grosvenor Square, Stoney brutalized the countess, forcing her to sign over to him her vast estates and kidnapping her off the streets of London and locking her up in her castle in County Durham to prevent her divorcing him. But she eventually got free of him and he ended his days in 1810 a debtor in the Rules of the King's Bench (see page 24).

Carry on along Grosvenor Square and go straight on into Upper Grosvenor Street. Turn first right into Blackburne's Mews, left at Upper Brook Street and right into Park Street. When you get to Green Street, you can see No 19 over on the far right corner. This is where Admiral Cochrane lived at the time of the Berenger swindle in the City (see page 54). Berenger called on Cochrane here before going to the City to spread the false news about the Allies' victory over the French. It was this visit, plus the fact that he had given Berenger clothes and money and appeared later to have profited from the swindle, that caused Cochrane to lose his seat in Parliament and go to prison.

Turn left into Green Street and then right into Dunraven Street. No 16, the second doorway on the right, is on the site of the house where 73-year-old Lord William Russell was found dead in bed with his throat cut on the morning of 6 May 1840. His murderer turned out to be his Swiss valet François Courvoisier. The motive was theft: Courvoisier had hidden various articles around the house and left more at a hotel where he had previously worked. Courvoisier was executed at Newgate on 6 July. Because of his connections – he was brother to the Duke of Bedford and uncle of the Colonial Secretary – Russell's murder caused a sensation in society and ultimately, taken along with several other incidents, led to the creation of a detective branch at Scotland Yard.

Further along Dunraven Street, on the right, No 19 is the site of the house where the beautiful 25-year-old actress Lily Langtry came to live in 1877 after leaving her husband and when her notorious affair with the Prince of Wales was coming to an end. Once ensconced here she had another affair, this time with Prince Louis of Battenberg, the result of which was a daughter, Jeanne Marie, who did not discover who her father was until she was 20.

At the end of Dunraven Street, turn left into North Row and right into Park Lane. Cross to the other side of Oxford Street and turn left. Cross Great Cumberland Place and continue to the beginning of Edgware Road (⊞ through subway). In the traffic island ahead you can just make out a circular stone set into the paving. This marks the site of Tyburn, London's main place of execution from medieval times right up to 1783, when hangings were transferred to Newgate prison in the City (see page 38).

Now retrace your steps the short distance to Marble Arch underground station, where the walk ends.

Westminster and Whitehall

Royal Mistresses

Whitehall, and its continuation, Parliament Street, is the broad thoroughfare connecting Trafalgar Square with Parliament Square, the Houses of Parliament and Westminster Abbey. Today it is lined with government offices, but in the 16th and 17th centuries it bisected the huge sprawling Palace of Whitehall, the main London base of the monarch from the early 16th century until its almost total destruction by fire in 1698. During the 1660s and 1670s, when the merry monarch Charles II was re-establishing royal rule after the Civil War and the Puritan interregnum, the palace was particularly notorious for immorality, gambling and pleasure-seeking, incredible extravagance and opulence, and a generally lackadaisical attitude to affairs of state. Indeed, at no time before or since – even during the scandalous Regency era of the early 19th century – has the Court's reputation stood at a lower ebb. The two main diarists of the era both had something to say about it. Samuel Pepys found that 'there is nothing almost but bawdry at Court from top to bottom. It is the effect of idleness and having nothing else to imploy [sic] their spirits upon.' And John Evelyn, having witnessed the king's brother 'bitchering' after women like a dog on heat, observed that the Court grew more and more loose with 'nobody looking after business but every man his lust and gain'.

At the heart of what many saw as the moral corruption of the Restoration Court was the king himself, with his numerous mistresses. Nicknamed 'Old Rowley' after a famous stallion of the day, Charles had a seemingly inexhaustible sexual appetite. Woman after woman passed through his bed – or he through theirs – and he is known to have fathered at least 14 children, possibly many more. One of his notoriously rakish friends once said he was the 'father of his people', adding under his breath, 'Well, at least, a good many of them.' The tragedy for Charles was that none of these children was legitimate. He did marry – for reasons of state an alliance was forged with the Portuguese Catherine of Braganza in 1662 – but his wife never managed to produce an heir. Poor Catherine had to exist at Court bitterly aware of her failure in this department. She also had to put up with having at least two of her husband's mistresses forced upon her as ladies of her bedchamber. One can only imagine how humiliating this must have been.

No one knows for sure quite how many women formed at one time or another Charles's seraglio in and around Whitehall (all his mistresses were entertained there, though not all were quartered there), but he had six main mistresses following his return to England in 1660: Barbara Villiers, Frances Stuart, Moll Davies, Nell Gwynn, Louise de Kéroualle and the Duchess Mazarin. Of these the two most important were Barbara Villiers and Louise de Kéroualle. The first dominated the 1660s; the second was introduced to Court in 1670 and remained more or less in command until Charles's death in 1685. The others were less important politically, but, in Nell Gwynn's case at least, perhaps equally significant emotionally for Charles.

Barbara Villiers

Described as at once the fairest and the lewdest of the royal concubines, Barbara Villiers was born in 1641 and married Roger Palmer in 1659. She seems to have met the king when she and her husband visited him in exile in Holland that year. At any rate, Charles set the tone of his reign on his first night back in London – 29 May 1660, his 30th birthday – by spending it in Barbara's arms. A daughter, Anne, was born the following February. Charles acknowledged the child, though Lord Chesterfield was probably the real father. After that Barbara's position was secure. It was well known that she knew how to keep a man satisfied, and Charles was clearly sexually infatuated with her. In December 1661 she became Lady Castlemaine when her cuckold husband was ennobled, and in 1662 she was assigned a magnificent suite of apartments in the palace after Charles forced her upon his new wife as one of her personal attendants. It is said that poor Catherine had a fit when she was first introduced to Lady Castlemaine. Between 1662 and 1665 Lady Castlemaine produced four more royally acknowledged children, and Charles showered her with gifts of money, jewels, plate, houses and land. But towards the end of the decade the king began to tire of his rapacious, imperious mistress. He knew as well as the rest of the Court that she had many other lovers – she was obviously a nymphomaniac – and he became increasingly angered by her outbursts of temper, which often led to his abasing himself before her in public. Eventually he pensioned her off in 1670 with the title Duchess of Cleveland, though relations of a kind continued to exist between them. It is said that in 1672, by which time she was living in Cleveland House, next to St James's Palace, he surprised her in bed with a young Guards officer on the make. The officer – later to be the great Duke of Marlborough – escaped out of the window with Charles crying after him: 'I forgive you, for you do it for your bread.'

Frances Stuart

Barbara Villiers may have been number one at Whitehall but she was not exactly without competition during her ten-year rule as mistress-in-chief. The first challenge came in 1663 when Frances Stuart arrived at Court to become a maid-of-honour to the Queen. Particularly beautiful – she is known to history as 'la belle Stuart' – Frances quickly caught the king's roving eye. Before long he was completely besotted with her, kissing her publicly for half-an-hour on end. But it seems she did not allow him to go any further, even though the relationship continued for four years. She may not have been overendowed in the brain department, but she knew how to keep a predatory man like Charles hanging on. Eventually she eloped one night from her apartments at Whitehall and married the Duke of Richmond. The king was furious, but later forgave her. The story is that only then did she allow him to possess her.

Mary Davies

A year after the elopement of Frances Stuart, Lady Castlemaine suffered a fresh challenge when the king began to take an unhealthily serious interest in actress and dancer Mary or Moll Davies. Moll, not merely an actress but also of doubtful parentage, was not set up in Whitehall but given her own house in Suffolk Street, near Pall Mall, furnished 'most richly', a grand coach to ride about in, and a valuable ring worth £700, which she was only too proud to show off. All this made Lady Castlemaine 'melancholy and out of humour'. At the end of 1668 Pepys went to the theatre and saw Moll Davies seated in a box above the king. The king looked up at her and so did Lady Castlemaine, to see who it was, 'but when she saw her she looked like fire'. Five years later (why did it take so long?) Charles and Moll had a daughter, Mary, who later became the Countess of Derwentwater. In 1675, when Mary was two, Moll moved from Suffolk Street to a larger house on the north side of Pall Mall, opposite her fellow royal mistress and actress, Nell Gwynn.

Nell Gwynn

Born Eleanor Gwynn in the Coal Yard off Drury Lane (see page 86), Nell Gwynn graduated from orange-seller at the Drury Lane theatre to leading actress in little more than 18 months. Her tutor and first lover was Charles Hart – actor, theatre manager and great-nephew of Shakespeare. Her second lover was another Charles, the rake Lord Buckhurst. King Charles, her third lover, whom she used to refer to as her Charles III, probably met her either through his crony Buckhurst or through seeing her perform on stage. By the summer of 1669 he was certainly her lover, because in the following year she produced the first of her two royal bastards, the Duke of St Albans. At that time Nell was living in Lincoln's Inn Fields. In 1671 she was pregnant again and in need of larger living quarters, so the king gave her a house in Pall Mall backing onto St James's Park (see page 127). Like Moll Davies, she could hardly have been accommodated at Whitehall, though she was often present there, amusing the king, giving as good as she got to other royal concubines – particularly Louise de Kéroualle – and yet sensibly staying out of politics. As a result she became the king's close friend as well as his lover, and stayed on good terms with him right up to his death, two years before her own. In fact, as one chronicler of the merry monarch's affairs has pointed out, she is the only one of his mistresses with whom there is no recorded instance of his ever having quarrelled. She also seems to have been the only one who was happy to call herself the king's whore, and her unassuming honesty made her many friends both inside and outside the Court.

That said, many scurrilous verses circulated about Nell – probably Charles's most famous mistress – of which the following is a prime example:

> Hard by Pall Mall lives a wench call'd Nell
> King Charles the Second he kept her.
> She hath got a trick to handle his prick
> But never lays hands on his sceptre.
> All matters of state from her soul does she hate,
> And leave to the politic bitches.
> The whore's in the right, for 'tis her delight,
> To be scratching just where it itches.

Louise de Kéroualle

When Frenchwoman Louise de Kéroualle came over to England on a diplomatic embassy in 1670 and aroused Charles's interest, French diplomats duly took note and arranged for her to return to England to be a maid-of-honour to Queen Catherine, with her own apartments in Whitehall Palace. The idea was that she would replace the Duchess of Cleveland, Barbara Villiers, as Charles's main official mistress and so become one of the main instruments of French control over the king. The plan worked perfectly. Louise fended the king off for a year and then allowed him to bed her at a house party in Suffolk in October 1671. The first Duke of Richmond, born the following July, was the result. Having been naturalized and made Duchess of Portsmouth in 1673, Louise – nicknamed Fubs by Charles – remained the dominant mistress in his harem until his death. As a lady of the bedchamber to the queen, she had magnificent apartments at Whitehall that were said to contain more than forty rooms. According to diarist John Evelyn, it was ten times richer than the queen's own modest abode, and yet it was still rebuilt two or three times 'to satisfy her prodigal and expensive pleasures'. Her rapacity was just one of the things that made her so extremely unpopular. Her Frenchness, her religion and her known role as a spy were others. Someone once succeeded in pinning this witty note on her bedroom door:

> Within this place a bed's appointed
> For a French bitch and God's anointed.

Despite all this she did at least remain faithful to her royal lover, unlike her notorious predecessor, the Duchess of Cleveland.

Duchess Mazarin

Louise de Kéroualle was seriously challenged only once, and that was when Italian beauty Hortense Mancini, a niece of Cardinal Mazarin, appeared on the scene. When he was in exile Charles had wanted to marry her, but her uncle, Cardinal Mazarin, forbade it. Later, after the duchess left the appalling man she did marry, she needed a refuge and Charles was only too happy to offer it. She arrived at Whitehall in December 1675, aged 30 but still voluptuously beautiful. Charles was immediately smitten, settling £4000 a year on her and offering her apartments in the palace. However, she played it cool and insisted on having a house of her own across St James's Park. For a while Hortense held the keys to the king's heart. Neglected and depressed, Louise de Kéroualle lost both weight and, tragically, the baby she was carrying, and retreated to France for six months. But she was soon restored to her customary position after Hortense transferred her affections to the Prince of Monaco, then on a short visit to England. Such was the romantic merry-go-round at Whitehall in the days of Charles II!

The following walk passes straight through the heart of the old palace area, and of course takes in many more sites associated with royal and political scandals, both historical and more recent, of which there has never been any shortage in Westminster.

THE WESTMINSTER AND WHITEHALL WALK

Start and finish: Westminster underground station (District, Circle and Jubilee lines).

Length: 3 miles (5km).

Refreshments: There are all kinds of places to eat and drink along this route, though the restaurant in St James's Park, about two-thirds of the way along, is a particularly nice place to stop.

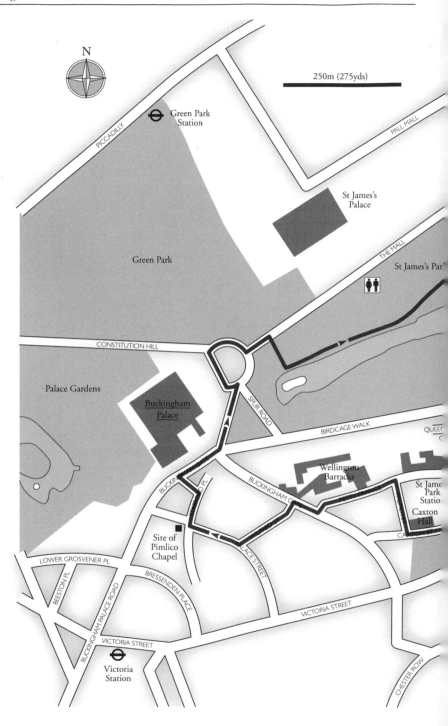

N

250m (275yds)

Green Park
Station

PICCADILLY

PALL MALL

St James's
Palace

Green Park

THE MALL

St James's Par

CONSTITUTION HILL

Palace Gardens

Buckingham
Palace

SPUR ROAD

BIRDCAGE WALK

QUEE

Wellington
Barracks

BUCKIN

D PL

BUCKINGHAM G

St Jame
Park
Statio

Caxton
Hall

Site of
Pimlico
Chapel

LACE STREET

LOWER GROSVENER PL

BEESTON PL

BRESSENDEN PLACE

VICTORIA STREET

BUCKINGHAM PALACE ROAD

VICTORIA STREET

CHESTER ROW

Victoria
Station

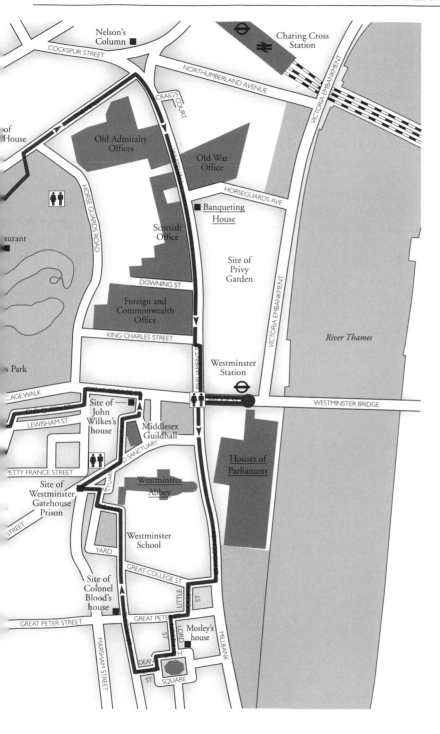

Take Exit 3 (Houses of Parliament) from Westminster station and turn left past Big Ben. As you walk past New Palace Yard, on the left, you can see the entrance to the MPs' underground car park; MP Airey Neave was blown up here on 30 March 1979 when the IRA planted a bomb in his car. When you get to Parliament Square turn left. The long, comparatively low building on the left, with the statue of Oliver Cromwell outside, is medieval Westminster Hall. The law courts used to be based here and Charles I was tried and condemned to death here at the end of the Civil War. (The walk passes the site of his execution later.)

Just beyond Westminster Hall is the public entrance to the House of Commons (see under **Houses of Parliament** on page 151). In the lobby of the original House of Commons (the old Parliament building was burned down in 1834), Spencer Perceval – the only British Prime Minister ever to be assassinated – was gunned down on the afternoon of 11 May 1812 by John Bellingham, a bankrupt, embittered and probably deranged merchant with a grudge against the government, which he saw as the cause of all his misfortunes. More recently Parliament has been associated with a whole series of scandals lumped together under the general tag 'sleaze', usually Tory sleaze, although Labour has not been entirely exempt. Perhaps the most notorious was the so-called Cash for Questions affair, in which Tory MPs Tim Smith and Neil Hamilton were accused of accepting money from Harrods owner Mohammed Al Fayed in return for asking questions in Parliament. *The Guardian* newspaper, which broke the story in 1994, also published details of a freebie Neil Hamilton had taken at the Ritz in Paris at the expense of its owner, Mr Al Fayed. Smith resigned, but Hamilton fought, ultimately losing expensive libel cases against both *The Guardian* and Mr Al Fayed. The case led directly to the setting up of the Nolan Committee on standards in public life.

Moving on to the House of Lords car park (actually Old Palace Yard), the main entrance to the Lords marks the approximate site of the house the Gunpowder Plotters rented when they planned to blow up the king and the whole House of Lords at the state opening of Parliament in 1605. The plot – a Catholic protest against brutal penal laws imposed by the Protestant government – was foiled when Guy Fawkes was discovered the night before in a cellar filled with barrels of gunpowder beneath the peers' chamber. After enduring terrible torture in the Tower of London, Fawkes, so feeble he could hardly climb the steps to the scaffold, was hung, drawn and quartered here in Old Palace Yard.

Carry on past the Victoria Tower and Black Rod's Garden and turn right at the lights into Great College Street. Then go left into Little College Street, right into Great Peter Street and left into Lord North

Street. No 8, on the left, was until recently the home of another disgraced Tory MP, Jonathan Aitken, who lied about a hotel bill (again at the Paris Ritz but not this time involving Mr Al Fayed) and as a result became the first former Cabinet Minister this century to be imprisoned for perjury (and also for perverting the course of justice – he got his wife to say that she, not Saudi arms dealer Said Ayas, had paid the bill). Having lost both his wife and home but found God, Aitken was released from prison in January 2000.

At the end of Lord North Street, look left along the row of old houses on the north side of Smith Square (Nos 8–9). Sir Oswald Mosley was living here in 1932 when he founded the British equivalent of the Nazi party, the British Union of Fascists. Mosley, a friend of Hitler and Mussolini, subsequently staged violent marches and campaigns, particularly against Jewish areas in the East End (see page 72), but the movement never took hold in Britain and fizzled out after World War II. Britain's most notorious blackshirt died in 1980.

Turn right now round Smith Square and exit right via Dean Trench Street, turning right on Tufton Street. Cross Great Peter Street. Westminster Mansions, on the left corner here, stands on the site of the house of Colonel Thomas Blood, the man who tried to steal the Crown Jewels from the Tower of London in 1671. He and his two accomplices might have got away with it had not the custodian's soldier son happened to arrive home unexpectedly and raise the alarm. Strangely, Blood was not punished; instead, after an interview with Charles II, he was pardoned and restored to his estates in Ireland. Why? One rather way-out theory is that he was actually put up to the job by the king, who was desperately short of money at the time.

Carry on to the end of Tufton Street and go through the gate into Dean's Yard. Halfway along on the right is the entrance to Little Dean's Yard and Westminster School. Like most of England's old public schools, Westminster was in days gone by notorious for its violence, particularly the thrashing of boys by masters. In the 1720s Edward Wortley-Montagu was beaten every day by his Latin master 'until my shrieks echoed through the long room'. More recently, one of the school's most notorious pupils was spy Kim Philby, who entered in 1924. During World War II he infiltrated, Britain's secret service for the Soviets and seemed likely to become chief of MI6 until he was suspected (by everyone but MI6) of being a Soviet mole. (He is encountered later in the walk as the Third Man in the Burgess and Maclean affair.)

Continue on to the end of Dean's Yard, turn left and then exit right, through the arch, into The Sanctuary. No 1 The Sanctuary, to the right, was the base of Mosley's British Union of Fascists when it was first set up, in 1932. Also to the right, the great west door of **Westminster Abbey** was the scene of a uniquely notorious event in British history when a reigning queen, who had just survived divorce proceedings in Parliament, was refused admission to her husband's coronation. The queen was the former Princess Caroline of Brunswick, the king was George IV and the date was 19 July 1821. Having had the door opened and then slammed in her face, Caroline, popular despite her notorious private life, returned home to Hammersmith and died three weeks later, no doubt partly as a result of shock.

Now turn left to the lights. The old Westminster Gatehouse prison stood here, at the junction of Victoria Street and Broad Sanctuary, from 1370 until 1776. Sir Walter Raleigh spent the night here before his execution in Old Palace Yard in 1618, and 24 years later it was while incarcerated in this prison that poet Richard Lovelace wrote his famous lines: 'Stone walls do not a prison make/Nor iron bars a cage.' Cross at the lights and turn right (Ⓣ left), then take the next left into Little Sanctuary, passing along the back of the Middlesex Guildhall. The Guildhall stands on the site of the sanctuary building in the precincts of Westminster Abbey, where in the Middle Ages, criminals – except those guilty of heresy, necromancy and witchcraft – could find refuge from the law. In 1532, shortly before the sanctuary was closed, there were fifty fugitives here, including one John Gonne, who had been in the sanctuary since killing a man in Westminster almost twenty years before. Sanctuary didn't save everybody, however: during the Peasants' Revolt of 1381 the notorious keeper of the King's Bench prison was dragged out on 15 June and beheaded in the City. Halfway along the Guildhall note the old gateway, the only surviving relic of the original Westminster House of Correction, built nearby in Tothill Fields in 1618.

Follow Lower Sanctuary round to the right and turn left into Little George Street, and then go left again into Great George Street. On the left corner here the Royal Institution of Chartered Surveyors stands on the site of the home of 18th century politician, journalist and Hell-Fire Club member John Wilkes, thought by some to be the real 'Pego Borewell', pseudonymous author of the *Essay on Woman* (1763), an erotic parody of Pope's *Essay on Man* (1733–4) and one of the most famous pieces of pornographic literature in the English language. Wilkes certainly had several copies of the poem run off on his printing press here: one came into the hands of the government and was read out in the House of Lords to a shocked audience. It's more likely, however, that Thomas Potter, the Archbishop of Canterbury's son, was the real author.

Carry on along Great George Street and turn left into Storey's Gate, then right into Old Queen Street. I believe (though it is difficult to be sure because of changes in street names over the years) that this is where that young rake William Hickey had assignations with Fanny Temple, a courtesan kept by an elderly friend of the Hickey family. One night, just as he was getting into bed with Fanny, the elderly friend unexpectedly turned up and there was a frantic struggle to keep him out of the way while Hickey dressed hurriedly and crept downstairs. After that they always made sure the bedroom door was bolted – surely a wise precaution!

Follow the road round into Queen Anne's Gate and then left into Carteret Street. At the end, carry on into Broadway and turn second right into Caxton Street. Just beyond the Stakis Hotel, the former Caxton Hall (plaque to Churchill on the front) was the scene of a murder on 13 March 1940 when, at the end of a meeting of the Royal Central Asian Society, Indian activist Udhan Singh shot retired civil servant Sir Michael O'Dwyer. The incident is probably explained by the fact that O'Dwyer was lieutenant-governor of the Punjab at the time of the notorious Amritsar massacre in 1919, when British troops opened fire on unarmed Indian civilians; but Singh said he had meant only to protest, not to kill, and had not targeted O'Dwyer specifically.

Turn right into Palmer Street and then left into Petty France. Somewhere in this street (my enquiries have so far failed to identify the precise address) the notorious disappearing MP John Stonehouse shared a love-nest with his secretary Sheila Buckley after they had met at the Ministry of Technology in 1968. Six years later, by which time he was head of a dodgy business empire under investigation by the authorities, he faked his own drowning in Miami and absconded to Australia. However, he was recognized there and brought back to England, where he spent three years in prison before his death in 1988.

At the end of Petty France turn right into Buckingham Gate and then left into Wilfred Street. At the end turn right into Palace Street. Up ahead, the Westminster Theatre stands on the site of the Pimlico Chapel, opened in 1766 by the 18th century's most notorious clergyman, Dr William Dodd. A society preacher who unwisely tried to live on equal terms with his wealthy congregation, Dodd got into debt and, having first tried to bribe his way into the fashionable living of St George's Hanover Square, forged a bond to raise money in the City. Forgery was then a capital offence and the doctor – after a great outcry – duly went to the gallows in June 1777.

Turn right now into Stafford Place and then go left through the bollards and out onto Buckingham Gate. Here turn right, walk down to the lights, cross left and turn right again, walking along in front of **Buckingham Palace**. Besides the relationship between Edward VIII and American divorcée Wallis Simpson in the 1930s and recent royal marital troubles, the palace has seen several scandals, not least that in 1839 when Lady Flora

Hastings, lady-in-waiting to the queen's mother, was believed to have become pregnant despite not being married. In fact, she was suffering from a fatal liver disease, a disease which duly killed her a few months later. Her family was outraged, the affair got into the papers, and Queen Victoria was severely criticized for her poor handling of the crisis. More recently there was the terrible summer of 1982, when Michael Fagan twice broke into the palace undetected, the second time actually entering the queen's bedroom and sitting on her bed. After reading press reports of the incident and its security implications, a man called Michael Rauch, the homosexual lover of the queen's police bodyguard, tried to sell his story to a newspaper. The bodyguard resigned just ten days after the second Fagan break-in. Rauch, ostracized by the gay community, committed suicide in a Notting Hill hotel room.

At the far end of the main front of the palace, Constitution Hill leads up to Hyde Park. Twice in the early 1840s Queen Victoria was attacked as she drove up here to take the air in Hyde Park, on both occasions being unhurt. The first would-be assassin, barman Edward Oxford, was committed to a lunatic asylum. The second, John Francis, was transported for life.

Cross Constitution Hill, turn right and make your way past the gates into Green Park. Both the Duchess of Cleveland and Duchess Mazarin lived in houses in St James's, ahead, on the edge of the park. Carry on to the lights at the entrance to The Mall. Cross here and go straight on into St James's Park, turning left beside the lake. In the 18th century the park filled with prostitutes after dark. Young rake James Boswell took frequent advantage of them, especially in the spring and early summer of 1763, when his diary records four unions. The first, with a 17-year-old Shropshire girl, was the first time he had ever used a contraceptive, which he found 'but a dull satisfaction'. A week later he 'strolled into the park and took the first whore I met, whom I without many words copulated with free from danger, being safely sheathed. She was ugly and lean and her breath smelt of spirits. I never asked her name. When it was done, she slunk off. I had a low opinion of this gross practice and resolved to do it no more.' Needless to say, he did not keep to his resolution. Two centuries later, on the night of 19 November 1958, MP and Foreign Office minister Ian Harvey was surprised in the bushes with a young guardsman. He was fined only for breaching park regulations, but he was disgraced nonetheless and never fully recovered from the nightmare before his death in 1987.

Just beyond the bridge (🚻 left), bear left at the fork and walk up the slope. You come out on The Mall opposite the gleaming stucco of Carlton House Terrace, built on the site of the Prince Regent's notorious white elephant,

Carlton House. This great palace, 220ft (67m) long, was built mainly during the wars with France in the 1790s and early 1800s. Vast sums of public money were lavished on it, despite the fact that millions were out of work and starving. Inevitably there were outcries, especially in 1816 when it became known that £160,000 – a huge sum for the time – had been spent on the house over the previous five years. Before it was even finished the prince, by then George IV, had transferred his affections to Buckingham Palace, and by 1829 Carlton House had been completely demolished.

Turn right now, crossing Horse Guards Road (■ right in park). Carry on through the arch, cross Spring Gardens and turn right into Whitehall. This final section of the walk contains a dense mass of notorious material.

First of all on the right, is the Whitehall Theatre, leased in 1944 by Phyllis Dixey, Britain's most famous stripper and fan dancer. She was once billed as 'The Girl the Lord Chamberlain Banned'. Opposite is Craig's Court, where courtesan Con Phillips was living when she published her racy memoirs in 1748. The memoirs were extremely embarrassing to recently retired Secretary of State Lord Chesterfield who, it turned out, had seduced Con when she was 12; he had refused to pay the £500 she asked to keep his name out of the book. Further along on the left, Great Scotland Yard was the original location of the Metropolitan Police's detective department, better known as Scotland Yard. In 1877 the Yard was rocked by a scandal equal in magnitude to the corruption trials of a century later (see page 110) when a number of senior officers were found to be in the pay of a gang of race-track swindlers who had planned to dupe a wealthy Frenchwoman with a betting scam. After a trial three officers, including two chief inspectors, were given two years' hard labour. A fourth, although acquitted, resigned from the force just a fortnight later.

On your right now is the Old Admiralty Building. This was the centre of an espionage scandal in 1962 when homosexual civil servant John Vassall, blackmailed by the Soviets since the mid-1950s, was exposed as a spy. His fall also brought down government minister Thomas Galbraith, who had been at the Admiralty in the late 1950s and who had formed a close – though it seems innocent – relationship with Vassall when the latter served as his assistant private secretary.

At this point in Whitehall, in 1843, Edward Drummond, the Prime Minister's private secretary, was shot in the back by Daniel McNaghten, a deranged Glasgow wood-turner. Drummond, mistaken for the PM, managed to stagger to his brother's house but died two days later. The case produced the McNaghten Rules, for many years the standard legal definition of insanity.

Across the road opposite the equestrian statue is the Old War Office. John Profumo was minister here in 1963 when the Profumo Affair – one of the most notorious British political scandals ever – broke in 1963. The scandal centred on Profumo's liaison with model and high-society call-girl Christine Keeler. Since she had also slept with Eugene Ivanov, an attaché at the Soviet embassy, there were obvious security implications. Profumo made the mistake of lying to the House of Commons about his relationship with Keeler, and had to resign on 4 June after the truth came out. He has since devoted himself to good works in the East End.

Horse Guards Avenue, covering the former entrance to old Whitehall Palace, runs between Profumo's old ministry and the **Banqueting House**, the only visible part of the palace to survive the ruinous fire of 1698. The palace straddled Whitehall, but the royal apartments where Charles II lived with his mistresses were behind the Banqueting House, between it and the river. Charles I was executed in Whitehall on 30 January 1649 after stepping out of a first-floor window of the Banqueting House onto a special scaffold. As his head plopped into the headsman's basket there was no cheering, only a 'dismal universal groan'.

Moving on, on your right now is the porticoed entrance to the Scottish Office, once the town house of the Melbourne family. Here in the spring of 1812 started the notorious affair between 'mad, bad and dangerous to know' poet Lord Byron and Lady Caroline Lamb, wife of William Lamb, future Lord Melbourne and Prime Minister. The torrid affair quickly became the talk of the town. Byron, however, tired of the jealous Caroline quite quickly, and eventually, with Lady Melbourne's help, broke off the affair, but Caroline remained obsessed with him for a long time, threatening to commit suicide with a sword and burning him in effigy. They probably last saw each other in 1814.

Further on, opposite the Cabinet Office, the relatively modern Ministry of Defence building on the left fills up most of what was once the private garden of Whitehall Palace. Pepys got very excited when he saw Lady Castlemaine's smocks and linen petticoats put out to dry here. In the next century, by which time the old Privy Garden, as it was called, had become public, Boswell took a streetwalker into the garden and 'indulged sensuality'. In return she stole his handkerchief, though swore she had not. Afterwards Boswell 'was shocked to think that I had been intimately united with a low, abandoned, perjured, pilfering creature'. Beyond the Cabinet Office you come to the gated entrance of Downing Street where the young Boswell was lodging at the time (he came here in November 1762). When Prime Minister William Gladstone lived at No 10 in the 19th century he earned himself a certain notoriety through his friendships with ladies of uncertain virtue such as Skittles (see page 132), and particularly through his 'rescue' work with prostitutes. Night after night he would go out talking to them in the streets, and sometimes he would bring them back to Downing Street for a Bible reading. Whether or not he ever had a sexual relationship with any of them is uncertain, but unlikely. He was warned many times about the personal and political dangers of his nocturnal activity, but he carried on until at least 1886, when he was 77 and once again PM, somehow contriving to maintain his reputation as a pillar of rectitude.

Beyond Downing Street is the Foreign and Commonwealth Office, known as the FCO or plain FO. Long before the Foreign Office was built in the 19th century there was a cul-de-sac here called the Axe Yard. The 17th century Poet Laureate Sir William Davenant caught the clap here from a black whore. In 1704 Titus Oates, the man whose lies fuelled the Popish Plot in the 1670s and led to the deaths of so many innocent men, died here. The FO itself is most notorious for the Burgess and Maclean Affair of 1951. Guy Burgess and Donald Maclean both became involved in left-wing circles at Cambridge University in the 1930s and were recruited as Soviet agents. Both later joined the Foreign Office and started passing secrets to the Russians. Maclean came under suspicion while working in the British Embassy in Washington. Back in London and working in the American Department, he was due to be interrogated by MI5 on 27 May 1951 but, two days before, Burgess collected him by car from his home and the couple disappeared, surfacing after some years in the Soviet Union. It turned out later that they had been tipped off by two other Soviet spies, Kim Philby (encountered earlier in the walk as a schoolboy at Westminster) and Anthony Blunt. These two were themselves later exposed as the so-called Third and Fourth Men in the Burgess and Maclean Affair, the shockwaves of which are still reverberating through the political establishment.

Whitehall now turns into Parliament Street. When you get to King Charles Street, cross Parliament Street at the lights and turn right. At the end (▓ in subway), the building on the corner with Bridge Street (now the Parliamentary Bookshop) was once the offices of the *Whitehall Gazette*, a front for an honours-for-sale business run by clergyman's son Maundy Gregory with the connivance of Prime Minister Lloyd George, who wanted to raise campaign funds: £10,000 bought you a knighthood, £30,000 a baronetcy and around £100,000 a peerage. OBEs, costing about £100, were specially invented; 25,000 were sold in four years. Gregory got a cut on each sale and became a rich man. The scandal came out in 1922 but Lloyd George, who had by then raised £2m, managed to avoid direct blame, while Maundy Gregory was somehow able to stay in business – at least, until 1933, when he was reported to police for trying to sell a knighthood to a retired naval officer. After two months in prison Gregory was silenced with hush money by a guilty establishment and told to stay abroad for the rest of his life. He died in Paris in 1941.

Now turn left into Bridge Street. Up ahead is Westminster Bridge. Late on the night of 10 May 1763 Boswell came here with a 'strong, jolly young damsel' he had picked up in the Haymarket. 'And then,' he says, 'in armour complete did I engage her upon this noble edifice. The whim of doing it there with the Thames rolling below us amused me much. Yet after the brutish appetite was sated, I could not but despise myself for being so closely united with such a low wretch.' This is just what he usually thought after being with a prostitute, and on this occasion he was repaid for his weakness by going home to his Downing Street lodgings and not being able to get in because it was so late.

On that note the walk ends, back where it started at Westminster station, just before the bridge.

Opening Times

NB: Some places – for example Westminster Abbey – stop admitting visitors up to an hour before the advertised closing times.

Bank of England Museum
Threadneedle Street EC2.
020 7601 5545.
Mon–Fri 10.00–17.00.

Banqueting House
Whitehall SW1. 020 7930 4179.
Mon–Sat 10.00–17.00. Can close at short notice for government functions.

Buckingham Palace
SW1. 020 7799 2331 (recorded information line). Summer only.

Central Criminal Court
Old Bailey EC4. 020 7248 3277.
Courts Mon–Fri 10.00–13.00 and 14.00 until the courts rise, usually about 17.00.

Clink Prison Museum
1 Clink Street SE1. 020 7378 1558.
Mon–Sun 10.00–18.00.

Cuming Museum
155–7 Walworth Road SE17.
020 7701 1342.
Tue–Sat 10.00–17.00.

House of Detention
Clerkenwell Close EC1.
020 7253 9494. Mon–Sun 10.00–18.00.

Houses of Parliament
SW1. 020 7219 3000. Ring for details of debates and select committees, and to arrange visits.

London Dungeon
28 Tooley St SE1. 020 7403 0606.
Mon–Sun 10.00–17.30.

Monument
Monument Street EC3.
020 7626 2717.
Mon–Sun 10.00–17.40.

Old Operating Theatre Museum and Herb Garret
9A St Thomas St SE1.
020 7955 4791.
Mon–Sun 10.00–17.00.

Rose Theatre Exhibition
56 Park Street SE1.
020 7593 0026. Mon–Sun 10.00–17.00.

St James's Church
St James's Walk EC1.
020 7251 1190. Mon–Fri
10.00–14.00.

**Shakespeare's Globe Exhibition
and Guided Tour**
New Globe Walk SE1.
020 7902 1500. May–Sep
(performance season) Mon–Sun
09.00–12.00, Oct–Apr Mon–Sun
10.00–17.00.

Southwark Cathedral
London Bridge SE1.
020 7407 2939. Mon–Sun
08.00–18.00.

Southwark Information Centre
6 Tooley St SE1. 020 7403 8299.
Easter–Oct Mon–Sat 10.00–18.00,
Sun 10.30–17.30, Nov–Easter
Mon–Sat 10.00–16.00, Sun
11.00–16.00.

Tower of London
Tower Hill EC3. 020 7709 0765.
Mar–Oct Mon–Sat 09.00–18.00,
Sun 10.00–18.00. Nov–Feb
Mon–Sat 09.00–17.00, Sun
10.00–17.00.

Westminster Abbey
Broad Sanctuary SW1.
020 7222 5152. Mon–Fri
09.30–16.45, Sat 09.30–14.45.

Select Bibliography

A full list of all the sources used in researching this book would take up far more space than is available here, so what follows is very much a select list and guide to further reading. The dates given are for the editions used, not necessarily the first editions. I would like to single out for special mention *Crime and Scandal* (1995) by Felix Barker and Denise Silvester-Carr. No student of the dark side of London's past can afford to be without this book, which is based on much original research into locations.

Allen, Louis, *Political Scandals and Causes Célébres Since 1945*, 1988

Ashton, John, *The Fleet: Its River, Prison and Marriages*, 1888

Ashton, John, *The History of Gambling in England*, 1898

Barker, Felix, and Silvester-Carr, Denise, *Crime and Scandal: The Black Plaque Guide to London*, 1995

Begg, Paul, and Skinner, Keith, *The Scotland Yard Files*, 1992

Bell, Walter, *Fleet Street in Seven Centuries*, 1912

Benewick, Robert, *The Fascist Movement in Britain*, 1972

Berkeley, Roy, *A Spy's London*, 1994

Blyth, Henry, *The High Tide of Pleasure*, 1970

Borer, Mary Cathcart, *Mayfair*, 1975

Boswell, James, *London Journal 1762–1763*, 1958

Boucé, Paul-Gabriel, *Sexuality in Eighteenth-Century Britain*, 1982

Bristow, Edward, *Vice and Vigilance*, 1977

Brown, Roger, *A History of the Fleet Prison*, 1996

Burford, E.J., *The Bishops' Brothels*, 1993

Burford, E.J., *The Orrible Synne*, 1973

Burford, E.J., *Wits, Wenchers and Wantons*, 1986

Burford, E.J., and Wotton, Joy, *Private Vices – Public Virtues*, 1995

Butler, Ivan, *Murderers' London*, 1992

Byrne, Richard, *The London Dungeon Book of Crime and Punishment*, 1993

Byrne, Richard, *Prisons and Punishments of London*, 1989

Campbell, Duncan, *The Underworld*, 1996

Carlin, Martha, *Medieval Southwark*, 1996

Chancellor, E. Beresford, *Life in Regency and Early Victorian Times*, 1927

Clarke, Jennifer, *In Our Grandmothers' Footsteps*, 1984

Deeson, A., *Great Swindlers*, 1971

Dostoevsky, Fyodor, *Winter Notes on Summer Impressions*, 1985

Goodman, Jonathan, and Will, Ian, *Underworld*, 1985

Gosling, John, and Warner, Douglas, *The Shame of a City*, 1960

Haldane, R., *With Intent to Deceive*, 1970

Hickey, William, *Memoirs of a Georgian Rake*, 1995

Hyde, H. Montgomery, *The Other Love*, 1970

Hyde, H. Montgomery, *A Tangled Web*, 1986

Johnson, David, *Southwark and the City*, 1969

Kelland, Gilbert, *Crime in London*, 1986

Kennedy, Carol, *Mayfair*, 1986

Killick, Mark, *Fraudbusters*, 1998

Low, Donald, *Thieves' Kitchen*, 1982

Lucas, Norman, *Britain's Gangland*, 1969

Masters, Brian, *The Mistresses of Charles II*, 1997

Mound, Andrew, *Heroic Hoaxes*, 1984

Murphy, Robert, *Smash and Grab*, 1993

Nevill, Ralph, *Light Come, Light Go*, 1909

Parris, Matthew, *Great Parliamentary Scandals*, 1997

Pearson, John, *The Profession of Violence*, 4th edn, no date

Phillips, Hugh, *Mid-Georgian London*, 1964

Reilly, Leonard, *Southwark*, 1998

Richardson, John, *Covent Garden Past*, 1995

Robb, George, *White-Collar Crime in Modern England*, 1992

Rumbelow, Donald, *The Complete Jack the Ripper*, 1988

Scott, Harold, *The Concise Encyclopedia of Crime and Criminals*, 1961

Shaw, Donald, *London in the Sixties*, 1908

Sugden, Philip, *The Complete History of Jack the Ripper*, 1994

Survey of London, various volumes

Sykes, Christopher, *Black Sheep*, 1982

Taine, Hippolyte, *Notes on England*, 1957

Tames, Richard, *Soho Past*, 1994

Thornbury, G.W., and Walford, Edward, *Old and New London*, 1880–86

Timbs, John, *Clubs and Club Life in London*, 1872

Wagner, Peter, *Eros Revived*, 1988

Webb, Duncan, *Crime is my Business*, 1953

Webber, Ronald, *Covent Garden*, 1969

Weightman, Gavin, *Bright Lights, Big City*, 1992

Wheatley, H., and Cunningham, P., *London Past and Present*, 1891

Wilson, Colin, and Seaman, Donald, *An Encyclopedia of Scandal*, 1987

Index